W9-BOO-365

Writing *from the* Heart

Writing *from the* Heart

TAPPING THE POWER OF YOUR INNER VOICE

NANCY SLONIM ARONIE

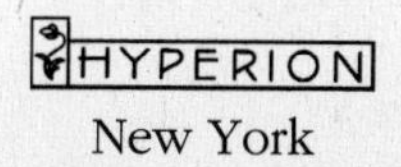

New York

Library of Congress Cataloging-in-Publication Data

Aronie, Nancy Slonim
Writing from the heart : tapping the power of your inner voice / Nancy Slonim Aronie.
p. cm.
ISBN 0-7868-8287-5
1. Authorship—Psychological aspects. 2. Creative writing.
I. Title.
PN171.P83A76 1998
808'.02'019—dc21 97–23990
CIP

Designed by Davidson Design

FIRST EDITION

10 9 8

To my mother, *Henny*, who gave me huge amounts of validation and always let me be me.

To my husband, *Joel*, who has been my teacher forever.

To my sons, *Josh* and *Dan*, who are my biggest lessons, my greatest joy, and my constant inspiration.

To *Dede Lahman*, who reminds me to live in the present.

And to *Ram Dass*, who taught me that there is one.

Acknowledgments

First, I thank my sister, Frances Curtis, for her extraordinary courage in living her truth.

Next, I thank my editor, Leslie Wells, who has the perfect combination of smart mind and warm heart, and I thank her eternally for her vision and her support.

I thank Israel and Asna Aronie, the best in-laws anyone could have. My gratitude goes to the whole Aronie clan: Mart, Alan, Steve, Sidora, Emanuel, Seth, and all my Aronie aunts and uncles and cousins for grist and grub.

I thank Shirley and Yuddie Wachtel for the continuity in my Jewish life, I thank Barbara Lee for free shrinkage and constant love, Judith Kaufman for her generosity and joyous spontaneity, Lorie Hamermesh for bringing beauty into my life and for providing me with a perfect example of creative discipline, Richie Hamermesh for his clarity and wisdom, Steve Kemper for his integrity, Susie Oken for her passion and for being my personal guide in nature, Niki Patton, my computer guru and fellow traveler on the path, Bert and Diane Quint whose generosity transcends thank you's, Ron Curtis for his perseverance as an artist, Mrs. Clarinne Grenfell, my high school journalism teacher who believed I was a writer years before I did, and Michael Stephanian for having been an unconventional, inspirational English teacher.

I thank Bob Luke, who opened my heart in the first place, Maryanne, Becky, and Lexy Ludgin, who listened and listened with their innocent, loving hearts, Priscilla Bright and Bob Verocha who share their light with me, Deena Metzger whose eloquence as a teacher and a writer gives me enduring guidance, Junko Yoshida Geisler who loved my babies as if they were her own, Drs. Barbara and Stanley Edelstein, who have been there every time I've ever needed them, Colin McEnroe who let me fail live on the radio, Deanne and Robbie Bosnak for their friendship, Carly Simon for taking me on, Marcy Brown who taught me patience and hard work in the garden, Kate Blinder who fed me in more ways than one, Sharon Mann for honoring ritual and family and including us always, Margo Datz whose imagination and poetry deepen my own practice, David Kalafa, for letting me all the way into his heart. Thanks go to Lary Bloom, who honored every comma and dash and gave me confidence right from the beginning, Jan Winburn who loves before she edits, Margaret Lowe Smith and Art Silverman for recognizing and nourishing the commentator in me, Jim Farrell and Steve Courtney, Wally Lamb for constant support and for being such a gentle reminder to stay centered and humble, Kate Taylor for her guidance and friendship, Dana Pomfret and Jeff Pivar for their music, Billie and Herbie Hancock for their generosity, Jim Martin and Linda Berg and all the members of the West Tisbury Congregational Church choir for letting this Jewish tenor sneak in and sing, to Peter Boak who taught me how, Terry Gamer and Sharon Mayock for making me look so good on the pages of MAX, Doug Wilson and Prue Berry for Rowe Camp, a place where god definitely dwells. Thanks go to all the holistic studies institutions, including Omega, All That Matters, Interface, and The Open Center for giving me space to teach and to grow, and to Phil and Scott Bryce for their brotherly love, to Ann Arsenault who gives me the sun in winter because she was wise enough to create her Women's Center in Florida, thanks to Pat Johnson and Laurel Lloyd Earnshaw, editors of *Aurora*, for providing a great forum for women, to Penn and Julie Kimball for their tolerance and support of the Chilmark Writing Workshop, to the members of the community of my town of Chilmark for being a small town with a huge heart, and to every single person who has ever taken my writing workshop, because you are truly my teachers.

Contents

PART ONE

Writing *from the* Heart

Part I

In ~~the~~ a Beginning

When I was a kid, I wrote a lot. It came easily and quickly. I didn't know if what I wrote was good or bad. I didn't think in those terms. I just wrote. I thought everyone could write. I didn't know it was a gift.

The fairy tales of my childhood always contained some sort of treasure as part of the story. Sometimes it came in the form of a vision; sometimes it was a magic potion; sometimes it was a set of keys. According to these tales, all one had to do was to slay the dragon or cross the ravine where the monster hid, or sneak the golden goose out from under the sleeping giant.

But it was always the *guy* who got to go forth and slay. The girl was always held captive somewhere waiting to be rescued. So when I became a young married housewife at twenty-six and felt imprisoned, I waited to be "saved." I had no model for knowing that the key, the magic, the vision was right there inside of me all the time. Besides, slaying a dragon looked dangerous, and I had more important things to do, like perfecting my potato kugel. No, that brilliant line that came to me while driving carpool couldn't have been my own; it must have been from Robert Frost's thing about building fences or Emily Dickinson's poem about being nobody. That was it; I was nobody. And since I was nobody there was nobody to acknowledge—no one to name, much less honor such a thing as—a gift.

> Inside you there is an artist you don't know about . . .
> Say yes quickly, if you know, if you've known it from
> before the beginning of the universse.
>
> —Jalal al-Din Rumi

Maybe, on some level, I knew I had a gift, but I didn't say yes quickly. It took me about forty years. But inside me there was an artist—*is* an artist. And this book is dedicated to the artist inside you.

"I've always wanted to write" is one of the lines I hear over and over in my workshops. "So why didn't you?" is one of the questions I ask. The answers range from "My mother died and I had to take care of my brothers" to "My English professor was always touching me while he was telling me what a good writer I was," to the most common one: "I never thought I was good enough."

I was in tenth grade when I won a gold key for excellence in journalism. This fourteen karat gold pin in the shape of a quill put a little glow on my struggling self-esteem. I wrote to my uncle, a professional writer in New York, and told him about my award, enclosing the winning essay and asking him for advice on how to proceed in pursuing my writing career.

Uncle Harry wrote back that I should concentrate on more realistic dreams like catching a nice Jewish boy who was on his way to medical school. "Girls don't write," he told me.

This is a sad story, but the even sadder one is that I accepted his advice as sound for many, many years. I set my course for one of the two remaining careers left open to women in the fifties—nursing or teaching—and of course with renewed zeal for getting the ol' M.R.S. degree.

I continued circling my writing like a vulture with Alzheimer's. What was that thing I was going for again? I kept doing what I thought I should be doing to get the doctor to sweep me off my feet. But what happened was the ground beneath those feet started shifting and the feet themselves started to go flat.

Finally though, I began to write (locally), to get published (without pay), and eventually even to teach a writing workshop.

One day I took about eight of my short pieces and rented a sound studio, made a short tape of my commentaries, and sent them to National Public Radio. I got an immediate response: "We love these pieces. In fact, we were thinking of having commentaries just like these on our show. The only problem is they're too long. We would be very interested if you could cut them down to two minutes."

Well, in those days I was so fragile that I thought that was a rejection. So I did nothing. And then, about three weeks later, the producer called and asked If I had those stories done yet. I was so shocked that

I stammered something and said I'd get back to him in a few days. I tried to cut the existing pieces, but I didn't know how to edit. It was just easier for me to start over completely. So I wrote about five more and called him. I said, "Hi, it's Nancy Aronie. I've got those pieces for you. Actually, I wrote new ones. Do you have a minute?" I was a nervous wreck. He said, "Sure, let me take it in my office." He put me on hold and all I could think of was that joke: "You put me on hold; I put you on hold; everyone's putting everyone on hold—but no one's feeling held." Finally he came back on the line and said, "Now, let me hear what you've got." I raced through two of them with my mouth dry and my heart thumping. He said, "Do you always write about your kids?" Well, it so happened that that was my life at the time, so I choked something out like, "Well, no." "I'll tell you what," he boomed, "why don't you send them to me on tape, and that way, I can give them a listen."

So that's what I did. I went and recorded the five new pieces and I waited for seven months to hear anything. Finally I received a poorly typed postcard, single-spaced, with just about the worst message I could have gotten. He wrote, "I don't know why these don't work for me, but they just don't. I have listened to them over and over again. You sound like someone I'd love to meet at a party."

I was devastated. I already knew people got a kick out of me socially. I already knew how delightful I was at a party. I already knew what a perfect guest I was, making everyone laugh and feel comfortable. But I was trying desperately to be taken seriously. I was trying to take my act out of the dinner party arena and into the world of grown-ups.

About two years later, my husband and I were in the kitchen listening to NPR, and there was a commentary that began with the words, *Jews don't hunt.* It was about a guy who married a non-Jewish girl. He bought a plaid flannel shirt, and his male in-laws took him hunting. The piece was funny, and had very much the same sensibility as my work. My husband turned to me and said, "Babe, that's just like your stuff. You ought to try them again."

And so I did. They aired the first one almost the day they got it and from then on, for a few years, they aired all my others, as well.

Girls write, Uncle Harry. They write it all. They keep nothing back. They publish books, they edit books, they write books. They tell their stories. They honor their voices, which have been silenced for too long.

So if your voice has been silenced for too long, let the idea of writing begin to take hold, to gnaw and to push and to build until, like a pressure cooker full of fresh corn, it will start to leak out in sprays of hissing steam.

Maybe you think writing is a nice place to visit, but you wouldn't want to live there. Or maybe you wake up one morning and know your writing dream isn't just a dream. But by then you have three kids and a job and a boss and a mortgage and not one of them has told you lately that your similes are as brilliant as diamonds. You're steeped in dirty diapers or angry memos, which makes it ever so hard to awaken (okay, conceive) your "writer within."

Now, if you don't know pressure cookers, let me be the first to tell you that they explode when you don't respond to their call. So if you don't want corn all over your ceiling (or words all over your pillow), you will begin to pay attention. You might start to doodle while you're on the phone; then the doodles will turn into two-line poems, then they will grow into *haiku* or start spreading into sonnets. Perhaps changing Pampers and answering e-mail is getting in the way of pouring your pearls out onto paper. Maybe they keep composing themselves right before you fall asleep or while you're sitting in the car waiting for the light to change. Or maybe you think corn on your ceiling could be a new Martha Stewart look—a sort of faux yellow stucco thing.

But if it's really in your heart, this writing dream won't go away. It eats at you. It nudges you. It whispers in your ear until you can't ignore it any longer. *I've got to start writing. I want to write. I have to get this stuff out.*

This is exactly the moment *not* to buy a hardback journal with beautifully handmade marbleized paper with a thin, silk, ribbony bookmark. This would postpone your writing life for at least another decade. These books are too intimidating. You cannot write a wimpy poem in this book. And you *will* write wimpy poems. And skinny stories. And going-nowhere narratives. And weak descriptions. And fuzzy plot lines. And confusing characters—in the beginning.

So, start by buying an ordinary pad of paper, a notebook that fits your life. In other words, don't make a big deal of it—but then again, you have to make a big deal of it. Are we having a paradoxical moment here? The point is: *Don't* have the architect come in with plans for the new writing studio. But *do* make a space for yourself. Don't order a state-of-the-art computer you don't yet know how to use (you'll spend valuable writing time learning about megabytes and megahertz). But *do* get a system that allows you to sit down and write. It's the writing that you have to get to—not the environment or the equipment. Both the space and the system are essential, but they must support the act of writing, not substitute for it.

As my cousin Bert Quint, former CBS foreign correspondent, says, "Writers write."

No one understands the wanna-be-a-writer phase better than I do. I spent enough years wanting. It was hard for me to make that transition from envying every author at every book-signing, secretly harboring the "I'm better" soliloquy in my jealous little head. But then, I realized, as long as I didn't write, they'd never know how great I was—and neither would I. Realization was motivation but still not actualization.

Now, let's say you reach the point where the New Year's resolution is finally beginning to be resolved: *This year I will write.* Writers write but you can write and not be a *writer.* Don't tell anyone you're going to start writing. The Zen paradigm says, "Stop thinking and talking about it and there is nothing you will not be able to know." So, don't think. Don't talk. Just start writing.

Well, that's simple. *Just start writing*. Like, just start building a new addition to the Louvre—something that blends with the old and doesn't take away too much from the new. I know—telling you to just start writing is ludicrous. But writers write. So my first piece of advice to people who take my workshops is: *Just start writing.*

Start simple. Start slow. Start now.

You can make the *simple, slow, now* a reality if you attempt something doable. Make a promise to write twice a week for a half hour as opposed to imagining that you are going to write the first three volumes of *The Elephant and The Jewish Question: A History of the Religious Rituals of the Animal Kingdom.*

Just find *your* way to begin. There are as many approaches as there are writers: Truman Capote wrote lying down in bed; May Sarton began the day by writing letters "just to oil the machine"; Hemingway got up at five in the morning and often wrote standing up; Henry Miller needed discomfort, and Wordsworth wrote *Tintern Abbey* entirely in his mind on a long walk with his sister (none of it was changed or written down until they reached their destination). Nabokov wrote most of *Lolita* while driving cross-country in a Buick on a butterfly-hunting expedition with his wife. John Updike works a regular nine to five shift. Toni Morrison rents a hotel room, gets there for sunrise and writes all day, and Jane Smiley has written in restaurants with her baby on her lap.

Julia Cameron's book *The Artist's Way* (which you should immediately run out and buy) describes a technique called "morning pages." Writers, artists, teachers, refrigerator repairwomen swear by them for jump-starting their creative juices. But please don't spend five years reading these inspirational books in "preparing" to write. Instead, read them, absorb them, revisit them if you need to. Then put them on your shelf and sit down at your desk, or lie down on your couch, or walk with your sister, or drive in your Buick. And remember, it's not where you're sitting or what paper you're using or what you're writing about—it's about beginning.

Rashi, the great Torah commentator nine hundred years ago, said the first verse of Genesis should be read as a subordinate clause (don't get nervous—I'm never going to mention the word *clause* again). It isn't a rigid "In *the* beginning . . ." it's a much looser, more forgiving interpretation when you translate it as "In *a* beginning . . ." So think of your writing as *a* beginning, not *the* beginning. That way you can start over and over and over as many times as you want. Just begin *a* beginning now!

There is one elementary Truth—
the ignorance of which kills countless ideas and
splendid plans:
The moment one definitely commits oneself, then
Providence moves too.
All sorts of things occur to help one that never
otherwise would have occurred. . . .

Whatever you can do,
Or dream you can do,
Begin it.
Boldness has genius, power and magic in it.
Begin it now.

—GOETHE

Yesterday's Soup

One of my favorite restaurants on Martha's Vineyard, The Red Cat, features Yesterday's Soup on its menu. You'd think everyone would raise an eyebrow and scrunch a nose at such an offering. But when the waitress comes over and announces the soup of the day, I ask how old is the soup. Usually the answer is a confident "It's fresh. We made it just a few hours ago," as if this is all it will take to ensure the order. But I know, today's soup is not what I want to eat.

Today's soup is water with floating things. It hasn't had time to blend its ingredients, so it is boring, tasteless, weak. But soup that has been simmering on low for hours and hours starts to take on a life of its own. The potatoes marry the carrots and the kidney beans ignite the chickpeas. The brown sugar twists the freshly squeezed lemon pulp around its fingers and the cayenne pepper pulls it seductively close to the edge. Yesterday's soup is rich, layered, filling; it's a meal. Soup needs time.

And so it is with our stories. We carry them around in our bodies, our cells, our souls, for our whole lives. When it is time to write, most of the work has been done. Whether consciously or subconsciously, these yarns have been cookin'. All we need to do now is add a spice (an anecdote), an herb (another detail), a leftover clump of saffron rice from the Indian takeout (a culinary literary risk); throw them together and turn the heat way down. Extracting the essence is what we're looking for here.

Soup is not like a soufflé, which you can really screw up if you're not vigilant. The pot allows more of a window for experimentation. And just because you're not following a rigid recipe doesn't mean it isn't honest. Creativity is *always* honest. Writing requires the same integrity as cooking. But you have to love the whole thing; you have to love the oohs and the ahhs when people take their first steaming spoonful, the stirring, the adding, the tasting, the leaving it alone, the coming back to it, the fixing, the "Oh, no, I ruined it!" terror. Writing is no different. You write, you add, you tighten, you leave it alone, you think, you take a walk, you call your mother, you fix, you sharpen, you print, you read, you hate it, you love it, you hate it, you give it time, you come back. And you begin again.

Writing, like cooking, begs you to trust your instincts. You can't be affected by other people's appetites. Sometimes you think everyone is so hungry they'll leave if you don't serve the soup right away. And you're tempted to get out the bowls before the exotic flavors have found each other. I know this temptation well. I have served prematurely, and my writing has suffered as a result.

Cooking and writing require the perfect balance of letting go and sticking to your plan. You need a trained tongue to evaluate the subtle changes that occur in your edible work of art, just as your trained ear tells you to take away an adverb here or change a pronoun there in your written masterpieces. Sometimes the soup is too sweet because you're afraid to feel your darkness; sometimes it's too heavy because you just yelled at your kid and you're feeling guilty; sometimes it's too spicy because of the things you didn't say to your husband that are stuck in your throat and are manifesting themselves in your soup pot. These strong spices have to be measured. Not with a measuring spoon, but with your willingness to taste, to sample, to test, to wait, to let the thing happen. It's hard to simply allow. It's hard to trust the harmony and to actually believe that your own wisdom and nature will kick in when they are invited as equal partners.

We're fragile beings, and we don't want to make lousy soup. We're afraid everyone will remember that the worst concoction they ever tasted, they tasted at your house. They won't know it didn't work because you took a chance with rosemary and cinnamon. They probably won't respect that you just had a feeling about the anchovy paste. They'll just remember they ate a lot of bread and drank of lot of wine and woke up really thirsty. But that's not what's important. It's about *process*, not *product.*

It's not about that glorious moment when it comes out on the newsstand, it's not about the people oohing and ahhing, it's not about the phone call from your old lover finally realizing you are brilliant. (Of course, that's *part* of it.) After all the energy we put in, we deserve the applause, the recognition, the acclaim. But if that's the *all* of it for you,

you'll always be miserable. As my painter friend Lorie says, "Fame is as fleeting as a shooting star." If you're thinking the moment of glory will feed you, I can promise you, you will always be hungry.

I had the good fortune to take an all-day writing workshop from Deena Metzger while I was doing this book. Until I met her, I had always run my workshop the same way. I made it safe. We laughed, we cried, and my students wrote. They wrote in my house, in my yard, in my office, in their cars, in the bathroom, in my garden—everywhere. And then we read. I had never really given them the option to do otherwise. I was always afraid if someone said no, then everyone would. Then, after the first excercise at Deena's, she said, "If you'd like to read, we'd like to listen, but I want you to honor the creative process because it's more important. If you're not ready to read, we will respect that." I heard her, and not only did I immediately know she was right and that I would now incorporate that into my teaching, but it catapulted me back to my early writing life.

Before I was sending things out, I would start a million things: my novel, my play, my collection of poems. The phone would ring, and all I'd have to hear is "What are you doing?" and I'd say, "Oh, nothing" (frightening in itself—calling my writing "nothing"). But then, since I had an audience on the phone, I would proceed to read whatever I was in the middle of or the beginning of or near the end of. So I'd read this thing proudly, and yet with a need for immediate gratification. Of course it had everything to do with avoiding the hard part of being stuck or, God forbid, finishing. If you finish—what next?

"Great," my calling friends would always say (at least I knew about reading to people who would respond positively). But then they'd hang up, and instead of going back to the piece, I suddenly knew I had to collect all the loose change I had seen around the house. The bank would be closing in fifteen minutes, and if I got all these coins in one baggie and added them to the ones in the car on the floor I could probably walk away with a solid—oh, gosh—three, maybe five dollars. And this, or something akin to this, seemed compellingly vital and completely valid. I don't know if I gave the piece away too quickly, or worried, How will I top this? or whether all I ever did in those days was just write for the recognition and for proof that I existed. Whatever it was, I almost never returned to the work. So when Deena Metzger said, "Honor the process first and foremost, and don't read it until you're ready," it was as if a public address system had shouted, "ATTENTION, NANCY ARONIE."

On the other hand, there are those who think so little of their work that they will *never* think it's time to let it go. Like soup, you have to recognize when it's about to reach its peak. Soup is no good when it's been sitting around coagulating. Potatoes get too mushy when they're old. The liquid dries up. Only a moment before, it might have been saved, not as soup, but as a great stew. But if you didn't catch it, it becomes glue; beige and gray with faded orange bumps. If you tamper too much with your story, you'll lose the immediacy, the edge. Overworking your work is a form of fear. At least, call it *work.* If I had known it was work, I wouldn't have answered the phone in the first place.

EXERCISE:

Write the one thing someone said to you a long time ago that still hurts.

One huge Vietnam vet biker guy came into the workshop. Up until this assignment he had written some pretty "lite" fare, some funny pieces. But when he wrote this one, he sobbed. His father had said, "Everything you touch turns to crap."

Another woman wrote, "Even a train stops." Her father had said it at mealtime when she hungrily tried to fill her empty stomach or, as she wrote, her "starving soul." She wasn't fat; she wasn't a hog; she was a kid who ate with gusto.

Here is mine. "You, the big one. Get out of the picture!"

Growing Pains

I am twelve. It is sixth grade graduation. We are gathered on the lawn in front of Rawson Elementary School. The dandelions are Crayola yellow, the grass is an electric green, and the sky is cornflower blue. The ceremony has just ended and everyone is kissing and hugging. It's my first rite of passage. There are six of us, all best friends. We are all lined up for group pictures. Our parents and our grandparents are snapping and smiling at their prized progeny. We are all wearing white. This is not coincidence—this is tradition. Diane is wearing a feminine white dress with appliquéd daisies dancing in the folds of her full skirt and little dyed-to-match pumps. Elinor looks her usual gorgeous self in a crisp cotton dotted swiss little dress with puffy sleeves. Susan's parents are the only ones who let her wear sheer blouses, and you can see her bra straps and her slip straps under her pearl-buttoned crepe dress. She wears pumps.

Barbara Cohen is the most sophisticated of us all. She is wearing an off-white linen sheath, and is the first of us to wear actual high heels. She already has her period, and she has the beginning of a teenager's body. We are all secretly jealous, but at the same time she holds a promise that we ecstatically know will soon be shared.

We stand with arms linked. I am so happy that I know from the inside out that this is the one time when my head taller and twenty pounds skinnier frame does not stick out. It's because we are all in white that I know today I am not The Freak. I am not the statistic that upsets the percentages on the height/weight charts of life, the numbers that invite everyone in for a look. Today, surrounded by my best friends, I am not the one who flies off those charts in the face of what any decent preadolescent girl is supposed to grow like. Today I have not broken too many rules. Today it doesn't matter that I am not wearing a dress, that I am wearing a skirt and a blouse and that my size nine feet are shoved into ugly old-lady flats. It doesn't matter because today is Graduation Day.

Suddenly a shrill voice pierces the moment, stops all the cameras, and slows the scene that is freeze-framed in my memory. Mrs. Cohen is pointing at me. "You," she says, "the big one, get out of the picture. You're spoiling the symmetry." I don't know what symmetry means, but I know that my mother and I shopped everywhere for a dress and when we gave up because the little girl outfits had waists that were too high and hems that were too short and the dresses we tried on looked like somebody's hand-me-down, we had to settle for a woman's white full skirt and a sleeveless white piqué blouse with a Peter Pan collar. I knew it was a compromise because my mother kept saying, "This will be okay, it's not really that bad. Don't worry, you look fine." None of those statements made me feel like I'd imagined Elinor must feel every day.

When I do not move, Mrs. Cohen repeats her demand. This last year I have already begun to hunch, to hang my head, to try to blend into the crowd. I am working on becoming invisible. Two years before, I had shot up seven inches in one summer. "Growing pains" was the way the doctor described my achy knees. "You're not supposed to grow that much that fast," he explained, laughing. "Let's just fatten her up," he had said, "and she'll be okay." My mother had forced a cheerful response, but they both sounded resigned to some really disappointing fact. No one saw me as a tender shoot reaching for the light.

Forty-three years later, I found the photo from the day a piece of my innocence was murdered. I remember how I had taken a scissors and cut out my head and neck, and lowered them to match everyone else's. I had taped and glued my head into place, thinking I had fixed that tortured Kodak moment. I became the surgeon for my own execution. This was the beginning of my becoming a writer.

Kathleen Norris (*Dakota* and *The Cloister Walk)* calls it the beginning of exile—a child in exile. I, like many others, learned early what pain, humililation, exclusion, cruelty felt like. I memorized it, and I held it as precious cargo that now infuses my message.

This soup took a whole lot of simmering: forty-three years, in fact.

This is not a one-of-a-kind story. This could be your story. The detail of the white sheer crepe with the bra straps showing through makes this one mine. You've got your own. Write it now.

Schmooze with the Muse

Every artist needs inspiration. And every artist calls on the muse in his or her own way. Dragging your Artist Self to the dead computer, to the closed piano, to the inert lump of clay can be torture. You may know how high you feel after you've done the work, but unlike having a baby, where you forget the pain and remember the miracle, you remember only the pain—and the miracle that was your poem has become silly, light fluff, a trite testimonial to self-indulgence. So, going back to the drawing board feels like writing the Term Paper from Hell.

That is why it's important that you create a ritual to invoke the muse. Just like sprinkling rosewater on dried flower petals, or mulling cider with cloves and nutmeg on the stove when you know your lover is coming by, you must spend energy to seduce her. I mean, why would she just come on over and plop herself on *your* desk, in *your* studio, at *your*

metronome if you don't even take the time and dedication to make a sacred space for her?

> The muse is both the deity and the messenger . . . for it is surely not only for our own sakes that the gods are willing to appear to us and breathe their holy fire into our work. The muse, when she appears, takes us out of our little life and thrusts us into the world.
>
> —DEENA METZGER, *WRITING FOR YOUR LIFE*

So if you can't write for your own little life, write for your larger-than-life life. Write for the world. Write as an act of giving—giving your authenticity, your integrity, your one-of-a-kind originality. It is your willingness to begin again and again and again that becomes an act of giving. Write as a practice. Write as meditation.Write as a gift to yourself. What muse would refuse ?

Of course, you can't manipulate the muse. You can't say, "Come to me—give me exquisite words that will fly off the page and melt the stone hearts of the editors of the *New York Times Magazine* section." The muse has heard this before, and she will shake her head and drive right past your house. "I have other things to do. What? I'm gonna force myself on a person who doesn't even put out a glass of milk and a plate of cookies?"

You can't fool the muse. You can't sit at your desk waiting. You have to turn on the computer. You have to take out your notepad. You have to have every intention of working. You have to have sharpened pencils, ink-filled pens. You have to have light on your desk. You have to have a desk, or you have to have a table. Or you have to have a lap and that lap

has to be readied. The muse has other invitations. Make yours attractive enough for her to know you mean it.

Meaning it is finding your process, trusting your process, and understanding that great work comes after good work which comes after lousy work which comes after no work. Meaning it means remembering this order. Meaning it means remembering that anything worth doing is worth doing poorly (in the beginning).

The first thing you need to do is to get in touch with how badly you want this. Is there a test for passion? Is there a way to know how badly is badly? Look over your journals and see if you've been repeating yourself for years in your longing to create. You may not have said, "I long to create," so you'll have to look between and around and under the lines. You may have said, "Nothing seems to fill me except when I go back to my painting class." You may have written, "Nothing excites me except when I write a new poem." You may have thought, *I heard a lecture tonight and was so inspired I rushed home and started a new design.* Pay attention to these words. They are your longing. Eating an entire bag of cheese puffs *distracts* you from your longing. ~~Sleeping with the wrong men is a *cover* for your longing.~~ Shopping for yet another basic black dress is a *trick* that makes you think you are satisfying your longing. James Hillman says, "Tell me what you long for and I'll tell you who you are."

Another test is to ask yourself, How much do I envy? When your friend gets a poem published, are you able to be happy for her? (You're allowed to have two emotions at once.) When you are really honest with yourself and you ask yourself what you'd love to be doing if money didn't have to be a consideration, does the answer keep coming up writing, painting, playing your music? Then maybe you do want it badly enough. It's hard to admit to yourself how hard it is to *want* something—don't add to it by making up creative obstacles. Make it easy for yourself to have a fantasy. Pretend you can have anything you want. *Now* do you want it badly enough?

Okay. You remember that you want to write, and you're in touch with the fact that you want it badly. Assuming that you've come this far with me, now you have to believe it is possible. Make a list of why it is in the realm of possibility. Don't forget what Richard Bach said in his book *Illusions*: "Argue for your limitations and sure enough you've got 'em!" As in, "I would have been a cellist, but my fingers were too big." "I would love to paint but I can't put up with the fumes." "I wanted to be an engineer but I couldn't pass calculus." (Neither could Einstein.) Now substitute your own *I would have but* . . ."

Next, you have to know that you are the only one who can make it possible. You can't sit at the counter at Schwab's drugstore waiting for the Creativity Scouts to discover you. After Lana Turner, no one gets free lunch at the soda fountain anymore.

There is no one universal formula that gets people to do their creative work. It's like what Rabbi Redman said about being ready for a more spiritual life: "God chooses one man with a shout, one with a song, and one with a whisper." Whether the muse is choosing you or you are choosing the muse, you have to be willing to try any number of approaches and to be open to any number of invitations.

You might want to have a sit-down with your muse: "Look Muse, forget taking a meeting. Don't have your people call my people. *I* am my people. And I need you. I promise to not abuse you. I promise to honor you. I promise to show up at the same time every day and wait for you. I know how busy you are. If I put up, will you please show up?"

Make a prayer out of it. Ask with humility. Beg with sincerity. Do what feels right for you. But do it.

EXERCISE:

Write an invitation to your muse.

Make your invite no more than one hundred words, but if it's only one sentence, that's okay, too. Then post it where you can read it each day before you begin to write.

Keats would most likely have taped this to his computer, but alas:

Muses bright and Muses pale
Bare your faces of the veil;
Let me see and let me write
Of the day and of the night

And in Dante's *Inferno* he doesn't take any chances; he invokes them all:

O Muses, O high genius, help me now;
O memory that set down what I saw,
Here shall your excellence reveal itself

Or mine:

Oh Muse Oh Muse
Please don't refuse
and please excuse
my unpaid dues
I'd hate to lose
your sizzling fuse
If you could choose
of all the Jews

this one who sings
the writing blues
I'd make the headlines
and the evening news
And finally be included
In
The Who's Is Whose

Before You Knew Everything, Everything Was New

I'll bet that when you were a young child you lived in constant awe and wonder. Everything you saw and felt and smelled and tasted was a first. And every first was recorded in every one of your cells.

But it's easy to forget what it was like to be that *present*, to be that *in the moment*, to be that *there*. Seems like the older we get, the more removed we become, and the more removed we become, the more it takes to have an impact on us. Turn on your television and listen to the news anchors as they report the most brutal rape of an elderly woman as she sat minding her own business in her one-room apartment watching her favorite soap, listening to their measured professional voices with just a hint of concern. There was a day when the entire community would have been outraged. Now it's hard to be surprised. The world out there has been lulled into a numbness, and a perverse acceptance of violence in our own lives has crept in unchecked. We almost expect it.

It's understandable that our personal traumas can shut us down in the heart department. When things hurt, there is always a temptation to say, I'm outta here; I'm taking me and my tenderness out of this nightmare. And with each public rape and each personal disappointment, we add another nail in the already firmly set-in-place emotional coffin, the one we have slowly tucked our selves into.

Reclaiming our innocence, returning to our emotional truth, is the way of climbing back out. Of course this "de-numbifying" requires *feeling* your *feelings.* And we all know what that means. HELLO, PAIN! And in the words of my Yiddish grandmother, "Oy, there's the rub."

As writers, we must be willing to feel our sadness, our anger, our terror, so we can reach in and find our sweet vulnerablity that is just sitting there waiting for us to come back home. Then and only then are we able to create the perfect weaving, the masterful mix, the ideal harmonizing of our wounds and our words.

The good thing about pain is that it serves the artist, it serves the work, it serves the growth of the whole human being.

You may query, from whence cometh this hurt, this perpetual boo-boo, this hole in the heart? If you were ever a child, you need look no further. The source of the pathology can be traced directly to the playground when you were cast as "Piggy" in your elementary school's version of *Lord of The Flies*. Or perhaps it was when your father threw your mother down the stairs. Or maybe it began when your uncle threatened you with your shared shameful secret. Maybe it was something as simple as two well-meaning parents who did the best they could—but their best didn't include listening to you, holding you, validating you, or telling you they loved you.

We hold our pain like a precious gold charm locked in the safe-deposit box of our heart. Never letting it see the full light of day, it leaks out venom, pumping the poison through our arteries, into our veins and onto our lives, holding us hostage with its increasing power. You can let it kill you or you can kill it. I say go in there—open that Pandora's box and set your artist free. She's dying (literally) to get out. And she can't emerge unless you give her back her rightful pain. She earned it. Now let her feel it. And sob from it and sculpt it and paint it and write it and sing it. And—what the heck—if she wants to—sell it!

So consider this your engraved invitation to feel the pain. But note: I don't invite you lightly. There are some things you must do first to prepare.

Make a list of people whom you know love you and whom you know are absolutely safe. (If your mother said "I don't get it" the last time you read her your work, that's a perfect clue that she does not meet these qualifications.) Make a list of all the good things you used to believe in (Santa Claus, the tooth fairy, that your parents would always stay married, that being a nice person was enough).

This is the beginning of retrieving that innocence. This is the beginning of chipping away at the concrete surrounding your heart. This is the beginning of great art—art that has at its core your bruised and bloody emotional muscle.

Feeling your feelings is a way to heal, and it's a vital ingredient in the recipe for living the creative life. Your innocence is your vulnerability. It's you at your best, it's you being real, it's you not trying to impress the teacher or the captain of the football team or your boss or your mother-in-law.

When you write your piece about the day your father died, access that fourteen-year-old girl who still comes home from junior high and dials half her daddy's work number before remembering he is dead. Readers don't need commentary. They don't need detached description. They don't need big words. They don't need imitation Alice Walker. They need you, with *your* language, *your* rhythms, *your* story. They need your heart.

That is not to say that using those brilliant writers as mentors isn't a good idea. It's more than a good idea. If they resonate for you, they are your teachers. They can inspire you, but they can't feel your pain for you.

The first day of my workshop, people come in ready to please the teacher, to start their stories with the best first line, to make circular plots, to tie up all the loose threads in neat little publishable knots, but above all, to sound literate, to sound intelligent, and to use proper grammar. So before they write one piece that might be sprinkled with *wherefores, therefores, or within whiches*, I tell them this joke:

> *There is an agricultural student who transfers to Harvard from a small community college in Kentucky. On the first day of school he is totally lost. He stops a fellow student, and in his hayseedy backwoodsy dialect, he says, "'Scuze me, can you tell me where the library's at?" The Harvard student almost has a heart attack at the destruction of the King's English. He looks askance at the poor lost freshman and says in his most perfect Boston Brahmin, "At Hahvid we nevuh end our sentences with a preposition." The agri-*

cultural student looks back at the Harvard boy and says, "Well, can you tell me where the library's at, asshole?"

Good writing is not about good grammar. Good writing is about Truth. So take what you need from your brain, the "IBM" of your life, which stores all the information: *He died at 1:29 on April 21 in 1977. He had a heart attack. Your Aunt Sadie's birthday cake was in the oven when someone called nine-one-one. He died before the ambulance came, and the cake fell.* Now go directly into your heart and remember how you felt that day. What was the temperature outside? How did you feel about what you were wearing? Had you baby-sat that morning? Had the daffodils that had been buds the day before bloomed? Did the fight you had with your sister when she accused you of warping her Frank Sinatra record make you sad or mad or both?

Now stay with those feelings as you enter your heart which holds his death not as fact but as wound. Feel the ache. *Please don't let this be happening. I can't breathe. How will I live without him? Who will give the bride away? My children won't have a grandfather. I don't have a father.* If the narrator's heart is not open, then we cannot be moved.

That is not to say that you should walk around with your heart hanging open. There's too much danger out there. Just find a way to make your heart safe for opening slowly, chamber by chamber, so you can get back to those *in-the-moment* moments.

One of the ways to remember what that was like is to watch children. Kids are always present. They are not planners. They don't cover up their misery; they *are* the moment. Watch how easily they can be mesmerized and delighted, disappointed and thrilled.

Nature is also a good place to begin. Nature never lies. She's a great teacher for seeing with new eyes, seeing for the very first time, *every time*. The Zen of seeing, or, as I have come to call it, *reseeing*, is exactly what a healing heart needs.

My friend Susie who has been teaching me to see colors in nature says, "God did it first and God did it best." We walk on the beach and she asks, "Where is the purple? Find the purple." Of course, I'm looking for blatant purple. I'm looking for a woman with a purple bathing suit. I'm looking for a purple plastic child's bucket. So there isn't any purple, as far as I'm concerned. She says, "Look at the ocean." My mind already knows all the color possibilities for *ocean*: blue or gray or, maybe in warm places, green. So I stand at the water's edge and I search for purple. She says, "Look again without the art critic defining ocean color for you." And by golly, I find it. It's a thin line between the sky, which is a blue black, and the ocean, which is a green gray. And I realize she's right: God did it first and God did it best. (I'm very discriminating when and with whom I mention the God part. When I'm with my scientific give-me-solid-proof-or-it-doesn't-exist husband, I say, "Look what those molecules can do," or, "How about them atoms?") But it doesn't matter who you think designed the thing. It's more about dropping the mental limitations that keep you from seeing it.

This spring, when the first poppy in my garden bloomed, I ran and got my glasses and looked down inside of it. I couldn't believe the perfection. The poppy was the reward for looking. (I looked, therefore I saw.) It was the choir at the Emanuel synagogue, hidden behind burgundy velvet curtains but sounding like heavenly lutes. I was eleven and I wanted to see the people singing, their mouths forming ohs, their eyes filled with love, but the poppy told me it was better to have imagined. What if they were bored? What if they didn't love the music? The poppy was perfection. Its dark center pulled me in further until all I could feel was still.

For years, I don't think I ever really *saw*. Some time ago, I was in the winter woods in Hartford walking with my friend Jude, my other guide to Mother Nature, and I said, "Look at the tree—it's exactly like the ones on the Christmas cards." She looked at me to see if I was kidding. I wasn't. She said, "No, Nance, the ones on the cards are exactly like the ones in the woods."

The other evening, on my walk, I stood still and listened to the birds. There were a million different songs, a million different arrangements. James Brown was there. So was Beverly Sills. Phoebe Snow was crooning, and Joni Mitchell, too. Bob Dylan was singing one of his cuts from that spiritual album that everybody was so upset about. It sounded perfect to me at six-thirty on a warm June night.

So I'm standing in the middle of the forest and I'm listening. And I'm seeing *and* listening for the first time. In between beating myself up for having been asleep for half my life, I have a memory. I was fifteen and I was watching Johnny Carson with my dad. The winners of the high-school birdcallers were performing their birdcalls. They took themselves so seriously. They were wearing purple and maroon paisley polyester pressed tight to their skinny round-shouldered bodies and brown acrylic flared stretch pants. The shirts were buttoned too high up on their necks and the pants were hanging too low on their hips. My father and I were making fun of them. We were imitating their stances and their strange sounds. They were stiff and awkward, so they were perfect victims for my dad and me to use as fodder. We had one of our best laughs over this.

Now I'm hearing the real thing and I know that I should have respected those kids for having listened so well and learned so much. They were honoring the birds, and I was evaluating their outfits.

How could I get back to that place before the judging and the labeling and the narrowing of my vision? It wasn't easy. My husband was the one who gave me a great lesson in perspective.

There's a little fishing village on Martha's Vineyard, where I live. The fishermen are fishermen; the shacks are shacks, the dead fish smell is the dead fish smell.

One night after our evening constitutional, I walked in the door and said, "That's it. It's over. Did you see how many BMWs there were? Did you see the whale ties and the pink slacks? I'm moving. The whole thing has turned into a tourist attraction. The quaintness, the charm, the Real is gone. We have to move. We have to find the next unexploited, raw, funky place. It's gotten too groomed. We'll just have to buy land in New Zealand or someplace."

My husband (wise sage that he is) said, "Nance, Nance, Nance—if we went on vacation in Cape Breton or in the south of France, or even northern California and we came upon this little fishing village and they had a charming restaurant by the sea and a little antique store and little shops with little gifties and fishing boats along the pier and people with funky, faded blue work shirts and people in pink pleated pants and conservative ties with whales milling around and some old cars and some BMWs, you'd be the first one jumping up and down screaming, "Look, look how adorable this place is! Oh, let's stay here." You'd be in "I-discovered-it-first heaven." He was right. I was stuck in the middle of my expectations of what it *used* to be like and what it *should* have been like. I'm always telling everyone else, "Don't should on me," and here I was, shoulding on Menemsha. Menemsha *should* be just like it was twenty years ago, or I can't appreciate it. He told me to pretend I'd never seen the place before.

Two nights later I walked down to the village alone and, sure enough, the place was charming; the little general store with the fresh vegetables on the wooden porch; the bench with an old guy sitting and reading the local paper; a new shop with handmade cotton sweaters and ladies-attending-the-croquet-matches hats. I got so into it I almost sent my mother a postcard from this brand-new town on this brand-new island of Martha's Vineyard. It would have read:

> *Dear Mom—*
> *Wish you were here.*
> *I finally am.*

It's a constant practice—this reseeing.

In the middle of writing this chapter I had to teach in Wakefield, Rhode Island. We happened upon a restaurant for our lunch break. I do not surrender when it comes to food. The Caesar salad dressing has to have Dijon mustard—not the country, not the deli, but the original. The cheese has to be fresh Parmesan, and the croutons have to be homemade and marinated in virgin green olive oil with many cloves of garlic—you get the picture. But for once, I told my husband, it didn't matter.

When we were seated and I saw the little basket of jellies—the mini-Smuckers—I mentally wrote the restaurant off. If they have these ordinary jams, they can't have anything even slightly gourmet-ish. My husband ordered clam chowder, and I said, "Oh, I don't care. . . . I'll just have . . ." I've never said "I'll just have." This time it didn't matter. This menu had no hope. This place had resigned itself to making fast food. Yet when the soup arrived, it was the best clam chowder we had ever tasted. I said, "Isn't it a good thing that I live with such an open mind?" We clinked our water glasses and had ourselves a good laugh.

Choosing to resee gives me the chance to retrieve what was lost; to gain the ability to re-envision. Like the children you have watched, like the child you once were, you can now choose to resee the world in awe and wonder. But it takes work. It takes practice. Even in the middle of writing about it as if I were some expert on clean-slate living, I still fell prey to the *I-know-all-about-this-place* syndrome from a simple little basket of jellies.

EXERCISES:

Been there, done that.

Do it again.

Write about an old place as if you are seeing it for the first time.

Write about a judgment you made recently that limited your perception of what an object, place, or person might have been.

The Winter of My Content: Giving Up the Comfort Junkie

In 1979 I read May Sarton's *Journal of a Solitude*. At the same time, I read Alice Kohler's *An Unknown Woman*. Both books were about older women who were living in solitude near the ocean. I had never spent any significant amount of time alone, and couldn't understand why anyone would want to. *I'm Running As Fast as I Can* would have been the title of my autobiography for the first thirty-nine years of my life. I filled every calendar square, sometimes with three events on the same night.

I remember my sister saying to me, "Don't you ever want to just sit home alone?" The concept of being alone was so foreign that I had thought defensively, *She just doesn't have as many friends as I have.* But somewhere in my wounded psyche, I'm sure I used the friendship tally as the barometer for measuring my fragile self-esteem. *Look, I've got three parties on Saturday night; I must be worthy.* I never wanted to be alone. I was the kind of person who walked into an empty house, turned on the radio and the television at the same time, and then, in case there weren't enough voices talking at me, called someone on the telephone to discuss the merits of steamed broccoli. I had never been to the theater alone, never eaten in a restaurant alone, and always created a social event in aisle five while contemplating the texture of Tropicana Grovestand orange juice versus the absence of pulp in the original.

And then, in that same year, we bought our cabin on Martha's Vineyard. The closing was in November, and as we walked out of the lawyer's office on Main Street in this small whaling village, I took a big gulp of the late autumn/early winter air and got a hint of what Thanksgiving would taste like there. And then out of nowhere, I said to my husband, "I'd love to spend the month of January on the island." I literally turned around to see who had used such an odd turn of phrase. I had never given the concept of isolation a moment's thought. The salt must have gotten into my peri-menopausal brain. Who was this person walking next to my husband, telling him she wanted to spend a month away from her children in an unheated cabin by the sea in winter? In one month's time, kids' cheeks narrow, their hair darkens, their little arms grow bigger, their speech patterns go into whole new rhythms. How could I miss one new syllable?

I had always been a comfort junkie. Camping out, if it were done in a four star hotel, was the only kind of camping I wanted to do. I never traveled without my down pillow. I needed to be warm, and I needed clean sheets. But before I knew what I was saying, "I need to be alone," came blurting out of my mouth.

Over the years, dangerous thoughts had surfaced and reeled through my head, like, How might things have been if I had waited to have my children until after I had some kind of idea as to who I was? But I'd always been successful at pushing these wonderings back down.

I had just begun to feel my feelings, and what I found was that I was feeling exhausted and pulled in every direction. Of course there were things I could have eliminated in my life that were no longer serving my soul. But I had not yet heard words like *serving* and *soul* in the same breath. Now, suddenly I was going to an unknown land without central heating, without a phone, and without knowing anyone except the real estate agent and the lawyer. (Now, there's a dinner party for ya.)

So, with a husband who heard me, kids who loved me, and a mother who supported me, I came to my retreat twenty years ago and spent the month of January on Martha's Vineyard—alone, with a woodstove for heat, spring-fed jugs of water and myself for company. At first I found myself wandering from room to room wondering what the hell I was doing there. The mornings were too long and too quiet; the afternoons taunted me with guilt-filled visions of undriven carpools and mounds of undone laundry; and the evenings were too dark and too quiet. I had hours and hours and hours of time. After all, it only takes a few minutes to make dinner for one, especially if you're baking a single potato—and you don't have lunches to make, baths to give, sheets to fold, bedtime stories to read, school clothes to lay out, papers to grade, dishes to wash, groceries to unpack and . . .

But after a few days of pinching myself on the arm and talking to myself in the mirror, I dug in a few layers deeper and listened. I found a whole unspoken monologue that had been rolling around in my head for years. *I want to be alone and find out who I am. I need to be quiet. When is it going to be my turn? Who are these small people in my house, anyway? And when is the* real *mother going to come and get them?* At the time, I was living in a suburb and feeling very alienated there; my younger baby was diagnosed with diabetes at nine months old and had several close brushes with death. I lived in constant terror that he was going to die; we had no money and I worked at jobs that had nothing to do with what I loved. I had shared my woes with my husband and my women friends. None of them ever seemed to complain about their lots in life. Now, in a rustic cabin surrounded by water on all sides, I wondered what I had been bitching about. Why hadn't I realized when I had had it so good? I needed a "perspective guru." And then I remembered the following story.

A man goes to the rabbi of his village and whines, "Rabbi! Rabbi! I live in a small hut. I live with my four children and my wife. There is no room for me to think. Now my mother-in-law is coming. I don't know how I will bear it." The rabbi says, "Do you own a cow?" The man says, "Of course I own a cow." The rabbi says, "Go home and bring the cow into the house and come back to me in a week." The man starts flailing his arms, but out of respect doesn't say what he is thinking (Are you crazy? Didn't you hear me? It's already cramped and impossible*). Instead, he shrugs his shoulders and goes home and brings the cow into his tiny house. In a week he goes back to the rabbi and he is practically hysterical. He says, "Rabbi, I'm losing my mind. I can't take it anymore. My kids are screaming, my wife is yelling, my mother-in-law is crying." The rabbi says, "Do you have any chickens?" "Of course, I have chickens," the man says. "Then go home," the rabbi says, "and bring them into the house and come back to me in a week." The man leaves in a fury, brings the chickens into his house, and returns seven days later. "I am about to commit murder," he moans. The rabbi says, "Do you have any goats?" "Yes," the man yells, "I have goats, I have goats, but I refuse to bring the* *stench into the crowded crazy house." "Trust me," the rabbi says. "Go home and make space for your goats. And come back and see me in a week's time." The man leaves, afraid that he will go home and do harm to his loved ones. He brings the goats into the house, and after a week goes by he drags himself back to see the rabbi. "It's an impossible situation," he weeps. "The goats are braying, the chickens are laying, the children are running, my wife is turning around and around in circles, and my mother-in-law keeps beating her chest. Me? I'm finished. I can't go on. My house is too small." The rabbi says, "Good. Now, go home and take the cow and take the chickens and take the goats and put them outside where they belong, and come back and tell me if your house is too small for your family." The man never returned to complain to the rabbi about the size of his house.*

But the size of my cabin wasn't the problem. My empty heart was.

Gradually I realized the precious gift I'd been given—the thing that most mothers never get: a month off—from everyone, including my type-A self. I began taking long walks on the beach. I began to read in the daytime. I read books sitting down in a chair, lying prone on a couch, hunkered down in a bed; I read books in actual daylight hours. The Reading Police never came; I watched the birds dance to the feeders, do-si-do to their partners, have a little nosh and fly away, choreographing a winter's ballet. I was never forced to wear a red letter *S* for *selfishness*, and in the market no one knew I had spent idle hours not producing, not mothering, not teaching school, not vacuuming. No one knew I had spent the most productive hours of my life not doing anything—just being. The perspective master was teaching me another way to experience emptiness.

After a few weeks, each of my sons, who were aged eight and ten, came separately and visited me. I loved that they could see their mom out of her cell in suburbia, alive with nature and surviving without "stuff." I loved that *I* could see *myself* alone with nature and surviving without stuff. At the end of thirty-two days, I had fallen in love with solitude, and—the biggest surprise—with myself. On the thirty-third day my husband came to drive me home. When he had last seen the house, it had been an empty shell, a rental. I had shopped at the two local thrift stores and bought old but gorgeous Oriental rugs and little lamps that cast warm, amber light from their tattered and water-stained shades. There were candles burning, the woodstove was glowing, and he arrived with a bunch of pale peach roses. We were shy and slightly changed. He looked at our real-estate purchase and, forgetting it was ours, said, "I like your house." It felt as if we were dating. All the marriage gunk was suddenly put on hold to honor this magical reunion.

It was one of the most nourishing things we all ever did for each other. When I got home, my husband, who had gotten to know the nine-to-five life of his children, had developed a whole new relationship with them. His kids had gotten to break many of the "mom" rules; they had gotten to wear dirty clothes to school, they had gotten to sleep in on the mornings after the school nights they had been to grown-up movies that ended too late, they had gotten a steady diet of Big Macs at a place where their mother had refused to take them. And they had missed their mom.

I had gotten to read, to write, to sit in silence, to watch and begin to identify and name my birds (Irving and Sarah never missed a meal). I had gotten to jog next to an ocean that went from gray to violet to green. And I had gotten to miss my children. I came home and I realized that I was not only, in fact, the Real Mother, but that it was a title I finally was honored to have.

* * *

And then I went to sleep. I forgot everything I had learned about the goddess Solitude, and I began to whirl like a social dervish again. In Greek myth, there is a river in the underworld called Lethe. It is said that if you drink from this river you will forget everything that was ever said and done to you. All I can say is, I must have had one helluva slurp!

Over the years the family spent as many vacations going back to the cabin as we could, but it took twenty years for me to return to the serenity I knew: that winter of my content. But three Septembers ago, when the beaches emptied and the colors turned purple and rust and the ocean went from gray to green to violet, and the light looked as if the sky had filtered all the summer car crud out, and every day became a clear day where I could see forever, I remembered Solitude.

The island delivered once again, quieting my frazzled soul.

I began the new retreat by rereading Henry David Thoreau's *Walden.* I looked under "solitude":

> I find it wholesome to be alone the greater part of the time. To be in company, even with the best, is soon wearisome and dissipating. I love to be alone. I never found the companion that was so companionable as solitude. We are for the most part more lonely when we go abroad among men than when we stay in our chambers.

And oh, was I happy to be back in my chambers. The first thing I did was stop answering my phone. It would ring; I would hyperventilate. It would ring; I would imagine it was Liam Neeson finally declaring his hidden passion for me. It would ring; I would hear Ed McMahon saying "Pity she's not home—all that money." After a while it got easier, and I got taken off the gossip-about-anything-now list. Soon my phone addiction subsided.

Solitude had begun to gently wrap her arms around me again.

I am convinced there is a direct correlation between not being able to create and not having time to fill up. When my students say they have writer's block, I ask them, When was the last time you had any solitude? Not loneliness, not sitting-in-the-dark-waiting-for-him-or-her-to-call solitude, but the you-don't-have-to-answer-to-anybody-but-your-own-heartbeat solitude. You can't give if you're depleted, and if you're running on empty, you have nothing left to give. Creating has a lot to do with giving: giving to yourself, to your soul, giving to the world.

I know it's easier said than done, especially if you have a full-time job, three small children, a marriage that is struggling, a mortgage due, or any variation on this frustrating theme called life. So for me to sit in my ivory island tower and preach how solitude is the savior that will cowrite your Nobel Prize–winner is hardly fair. Maybe there's a compromise in there for you. How about from a month *away* to twenty minutes *unavailable*? Sue Benchley, who wrote the beautiful book, *Every Day Sacred*, calls them "little sabbaths." Take a little sabbath every day.

* * *

I have always been an "either or" gal. If I couldn't have a studio, then I couldn't be expected to do art. Either I did it *exactly* the way my limited mind had pictured it, or I didn't do it at all. So I eliminated throngs of in-between possibilities. So, do as I say, not as I spent years doing. If you can't get exactly what you want at that moment, then you need to take advantage of what you do have now. If you can't go to Maho Bay and scuba dive, then go sit in the park and watch the old men playing chess. If you can't get the time to go to the park, then go down to the cool basement or up to the sunny attic and sit and stare into the darkness or the light. But make some compromise so your soul gets some silence.

I was never going to just sit down voluntarily. So the universe collaborated with me and we broke my wrist. I think that event shook the concrete of my frozen foundation. I was forced to literally sit down and smell the bandages on my aching hand. It succeeded in slowing me down and pulling me out of my self-inflicted narrow-vision prison.

One day, while I was out of commission, I sat in my chair looking out at a tree in my backyard, a tree that I had never noticed before. But something was wrong with this tree. It was holding up our hammock that I never used. Its leaves were mostly dried up and dead. It had become a post, a dying post. I sat holding my crippled wrist realizing that we had killed that tree. We had wrapped wire around and around its bark so that we could lie in the sun and relax. Every day I would sit in the window and look down at the dead tree. One day when I was feeling well enough to go out, I walked up to the tree, touched its wounds, and stood there apologizing out loud. "I just never knew you were alive," I cried. I hugged her and felt her scars, saw her sap like dark dried blood, and asked again for forgiveness. I told her I never knew *I* was alive, either.

What I know now is that if I hadn't broken my wrist, none of this awareness or healing would have taken place. I knew my broken wrist was more than a fair trade. After that day, I spent a few more weeks recovering. I watched the golden maple leaves falling with no direction. Just each leaf allowing itself to float to its random destination. What is it about us humans that makes us so *end-result* driven? Why can't we (pardon the well-frayed phrase) just go with the flow? Why does there always have to be a winner? Why do we always have to get someplace? Why can't *wherever you go, there you are* be enough? In his best-selling book of the same name, Jon Kabat-Zinn says, "Have you ever noticed that there is no running away from anything? . . . The romantic notion is that if it's no good over here, you have only to go over there and things will be different. If this job is no good, change jobs. If this wife is no good, change wives. If this town is no good, change towns. If these children are a problem, leave them for other people to look after. The underlying thinking is that the reason for your troubles is outside of you—in the location, in others, in the circumstances. . . . The trouble with this way of seeing is that it conveniently ignores the fact that you carry your head and your heart and what some would call your 'karma' around with you. You cannot escape yourself, try as you might. . . . We don't understand that it is actually possible to attain clarity, understanding, and transformation right in the middle of what is here and now." Why had I never made time to do this? A battle was being waged between my busy busy mind and the emptiness that held my truth.

Of course, not everyone responds in the same way to quiet. Some city folk say they can't sleep in the country. They miss the garbage trucks grinding, the street sweeper cleaning, the sirens blaring. Maybe they've learned how to incorporate those cacophonous sounds into their dreams, and they are in harmony with those rhythms. I can't tell you *where* your stillness is. I can only tell you to look until you find it.

So, for those of you who are speeding down the track at a billion miles per hour, see if you can try this solution. Find a place you can return to unheeded. A place that won't be discovered and tampered with. Make an altar for yourself. Leave it empty to help you invoke a sense of simplicity, or put a picture of someone you love: a teacher, a mentor, your godchild, anyone who is a guaranteed heart opener. Add a candle or a whole bunch. There are scented candles with healing aromatherapies, there are candles designed to help open specific chakras, and there are just-plain-candle candles. Take a piece of antique lace or old silk or new velvet and create a tiny space that is yours. Don't do what I used to do—throw the baby out with the bathwater. *I don't have a room of my own, therefore I can't write.* This is a crock of Wheatena gone bad. A "room of your own" can be a *corner* of your own. Take what you can get, and work with it. You *can* do what you can do. It will feed you, and, interestingly, it might feed you as much as the trip to the Caribbean.

It's not your travel plans that have to change; it's your intention that has to change. It's all in the intention: I want to write, so I *will* write. I want to paint, so I *will* paint. I want to make music, so I *will* make music. Writers write, painters paint, musicians make music. And don't forget—none of it has to be good; it just has to be. I know now that I cannot write if I don't get the solitude I need. I finally understand that not only is silence golden, but solitude for artists is essential.

Now, repeat after me: *I need this space. I deserve this space. I will honor myself and take this space.*

EXERCISE:

Decide where the "room" of your own will be. Put one or two special things there as soon as you pick the place. Spend whatever spare minutes you have this week getting the space ready.

Grande Boca (Big Mouth) Comes to Rest

Thomas Moore, one of my favorite teachers and a former monk who wrote *Care of the Soul* and *Soul Mates*, says he thinks he took a vow of silence in utero. I think I took a vow of constant conversation.

Listening. Now, there's a concept. Listening is a skill they forgot to add to the curriculum in elementary school. *I* certainly never took the course. And as an attention-deprived kid, listening would have interrupted my constant aria: *Love me, please, somebody love me.* As an adult, I knew I wanted to be a better listener. I knew who the good listeners were.

When I was engaged in any dialogue with any person, I would get the gist—or at least *think* I got the gist—of what the other person was saying, then I would finish their sentences. Half the time, my endings had nothing to do with their beginnings. I would give advice on something about which I assumed they were just about to ask. I was so afraid "my listener" would leave; I became a speed demon, anticipating his response so I could fire back an answer and regain control of the volley (my tennis game should have been that good). Most people were too polite to stop me once I was on my Ann Landers roll. I would sympathize and empathize and believe that I was being such a good friend. But I heard nothing, so they got what I chose to give them, not necessarily what they needed to hear. My heart was in the right place, but my mind was on fast forward and there was no "pause" button.

I had always been afraid of silences. If there was a lull in the conversation, you could always count on me to jump in and make everyone comfortable. Truth be known, it was my own discomfort: Silence meant you could get yelled at, someone could notice your buck teeth, someone could discover you weren't as smart as you wanted them to believe. Silence could give them time to find your emotional Achilles heel.

When I did listen, it was only when I needed something. I mean, I could always hear when I was waiting for a boy to say I love you. I could always hear when the teacher told me I had written a great essay. I could always hear when my father said, "Good girl." But that was listening with an agenda, listening for a clue that I existed. Never just listening. Ram Dass says there has to be an emptiness in order to hear. No wonder I never heard. I was empty, but not the Zen kind.

Reading Thomas Moore taught me that listening could be learned. As a young seminary student of nineteen, Moore went to his teacher and told him he'd been reading a book on meditation. It said that the best way to meditate was to have a conversation with Christ. Moore told his teacher he was trying, but that he was doing all the talking. The teacher told him that he should just keep listening. So he did. After reading Jung, Rilke, Ficino, Yeats, and Dickinson, Moore says he finally learned how to listen meditatively. It took him thirty years.

So here was this wisest of wise men admitting how hard it was for him to learn how to stop talking. If I don't quiet down, it looks like I'll be over ninety by the time my kids get to have a real dialogue with me.

About a year ago, I was in the car with my husband. We were in Waltham, Massachusetts, driving in rush-hour traffic, and I was delivering a monologue to the poor trapped man. The litany went like this:

> *"I need to listen. I have reached a point in my life where I know now I have to learn to listen. I need to just sit and empty out—listen to people when they talk to each other—you know, be a fly on the wall. . . . just listen to friends when they talk, not offer any remarks, any solutions. . . . I know this from the bottom of my being. . . . I don't know what I'm asking you to do, maybe when we're at a social thing, maybe you could just look across the room and remind me with a wink or a grin or . . . maybe if you see me talking too much you could mouth the words* shut up*. . . . Of course,* shut up *is really harsh, so* shut up *is no good. . . . What signal could we come up with when I'm talking nonstop? You know, some kind of reminder that I'm doing it again . . . our own private reminder . . . but it can't be a killer reminder, it has to be a nontoxic reminder . . . a code phrase. Or maybe you could start singing 'Silent Night' or something. I guess that would seem odd though, if it happens to be in the middle of July. . . ."*

Suddenly we came up to a red light. The car stopped moving and I stopped talking. There across the street, directly in front of us, was a huge building with a massive neon sign looming overhead. It read GRANDE BOCA, which, if your Spanish is rusty, means "big mouth." We burst out laughing.

The timing was perfect. I said, "God has such a great sense of humor," but then I remembered how hard it is for my husband to "do" God, so I added, "Or it's just a coincidence." We had our first moment of silence since we had gotten into the car.

When you start to listen, you will hear all kinds of surprises. You might hear what the Quakers call the "still small voice within." You might hear nature alive and teeming with sound. You might hear your cat wheezing. You might hear your resident mice chewing. You might hear your refrigerator humming. You might hear your friend, who "gave up smoking," taking a big inhale on the other end of the phone. You might finally hear your own self.

You will hear your heart—not its beat, but its message, its history, its yearning, its connection to you, its plea for silence. Listening will let you hear your truth that has been trying to get through for years, the one we couldn't hear through the din of our spinning heads, as we were so busy rearranging the dinner menu alphabetically: arugula, beans, candied sweet potatoes, duck *a l'orange* (ooh, not a bad meal). See where this kind of useless thinking can take you? I'm already salivating and making reservations at a restaurant I can't afford and nary a moment of listening has taken place.

When you listen, you can hear the secrets you carry, the ones you need to acknowlege so you can put yourself back together. The missing pieces. The notes in between the written notes on the page. Dr. Wayne Dyer, who wrote *Your Erroneous Zones* and *You'll See It When You Believe It*, says the music is not in the notes, it's in the silence between the notes. Deena Metzger says after you write your first draft, open up the story like an accordion and write what you left out the first time. My friend Bob Dente says that when he teaches painting, he tells his students that the negative space, the backround to the thing they're painting, is just as important as the object they paint.

So do the same thing with your ears—open them up like an accordion, listen for the unobvious, the negative spaces. And then maybe you will hear instructions gently guiding you to your next destination. And if you really listen after you've already listened, you will receive the map that will get you there. That's the stuff you will hear when you begin to listen.

Three of my women friends and I were discussing how, when we were younger, we thought guys who were athletes or gorgeous or brilliant were turn-ons. Each one of us agreed that now all we want is someone who listens. My friend Barbara says listening is love.

Writers need to listen. Most of your characters are right inside you waiting to be fleshed out, shaped, brought to life. But the ones who are missing are walking the streets in your neighborhood, are sitting having a cappuccino next to you at Starbucks, are standing in front of you in the express line at the supermarket. Know that they are part of your work, your material, your ticket to someone else's reality. Start to become Harriet the Spy. Confer upon yourself a doctorate of human behavior and treat life as if it's the best play you ever got box seats for. The dude in the tights said it best: "All the world's a stage." He may not have known a whole lot about footwear fashion, but he got the human condition thing down.

There was a woman in one of my workshops who kept writing about how miserable she was in her job. Every week she would come in with another journal entry complaining about how much she hated her boss and her coworkers. She was so caught up in her misery in her drab office with her mean boss. She said it was zapping all her energy, and when she got home, she just couldn't write. And the more she worked in this horrible situation, the more she longed to quit and become a writer. But she knew she couldn't afford to leave.

I knew she was sitting on a gold mine, so I asked her to describe her boss. "Ughhh, please," she said. "His monogrammed shirts from Hong Kong are bursting at the seams. He was thinner and nicer when he was poorer." "Beautiful!" I cried. She looked confused, and I asked her to tell me more.

The man was vicious his voice hadn't dropped, so she assumed neither had his testicles. She became more and more animated. "I hate my office," she said, "the worn stairs, the musty smell, the greasy banisters, the creaky elevator." I said, "Perfect!" She was starting to get it. I said, "Carol, you are in a place where you are privy to information no other other writer is privy to. No other writer has this boss in this building at this time."

So this was Carolyn's story. She didn't need to bitch about it; she needed to write it. And we wanted to read it. We wanted to hate that boss and to see the rest of the victims under his reign. We wanted the narrator to write herself into her freedom. She might have written a wonderful story of a woman who murders her boss and inherits the business, or she might have written the solution that gets her out of there—or both.

From now on, listen to everyone. Everywhere you can, get your ears on. Don't let one single piece of information go by you. Don't take anything personally again, except to secretly thank obnoxious people for giving you such good stuff. Take your writer to work with you. Don't wait till you get home to let her out. Use your life. It's the best unsold manuscript around. You can transform your personal drudgery into a work of art. Look at what Kafka did while working as a government clerk. And Wallace Stevens sold insurance, for God's sake!

Next time you are in the market in line with your cilantro wilting and reminding yourself that your husband thinks it tastes like soap, look around and see all the characters that want to be included in your story. Pick the ones you want. They're all gifts. Go ahead. Pick the redhead in front of you. Listen to how she talks to the woman at the cash register. Is she opening the Häagen-Dazs coffee ice cream container and pulling the plastic cover off with her teeth? Watch how she hands the clerk her coupons. Are they organized in a box? Are they neatly folded in her wallet? Is she frantically ripping them from the flyer right there, oblivious to the fact that the line is growing like an unchecked mole? Does she know the shopper behind her is balancing six items with two babies, while she's trying to get forty cents off her Pepperidge Farm mint Milano cookies? Does she smile and laugh a nervous laugh and apologize or does she act like you're not there? Listen to what she says. If she apologizes, notice how patient you become. If she ignores you, notice how agitated you become.

Watch the rest of the line. Are they sneaking disgusted, knowing glances at each other? Is someone rolling his eyes heavenward? Watch how strangers bond over mutual judgment of one disorganized shopper. Now, when she leaves, listen to who says what. There will always be one person who thinks you're still having the meeting. Everyone else just wants to get home, but this guy had a moment of belonging, and he wants to sustain it. Listen to the tension. It is a delicious piece of writing. And you thought you were just running in and grabbing some skim milk.

Once I began learning to listen, the universe began to cooperate. A friend of mine faxes me the Torah reading every Friday night just before sundown. I have come to take the ritual quite seriously. I stop everything and I light the candles and then I sit and read the portion of the Talmud, the lesson of the week. One particular Friday, I had been doing all my white cotton laundry because I was getting ready to leave for Florida. Our water has a high content of iron and rust in it, and I'm always frustrated at the variations of white that I get. My once-bright white T-shirts come out in combinations of eggshell yellow and beige, and gray and off-white. The *parsha*, the portion, that week discussed how certain priestly garments were designed to be more than just beautiful, that in fact they were designed to increase reverence for the temple, that they had deep symbolic and mystical significance. It explained that the seventy-two bells and pomegranates on the hems of the robes worn by the high priests were a reminder of the seventy-two shades of white that confirmed that a person had *Tzara'as*, the disease which, in ancient days, afflicted only those who spoke *Loshon Hara* (public gossip and slander). This was what I was reading one pleasant evening with seventy-two shades of summer whites ready to be stuffed into my bags heading south. And I had to confront the Loshon Hara factor. As if this were not bad enough, the Talmud went on to explain that the bells represented the spoken voice and the pomegranates the closed mouth. It said the Torah teaches us that we should be silent twice as much as we speak—one bell between two pomegranates.

Oh, thank you, great wise fax god, for bringing me yet another reminder.

The listening thing is as good as done.

EXERCISE:

Eavesdrop all day. Keep your notepad near you and write down the lines that hit you. Go home or to your favorite writing spot and start your piece with the line you love most. You are not looking for Shakespeare.You are looking for inspiration. You are looking for a line that resonates. It could be as simple as "I waited for him all night."

Write a character sketch about someone at work. What is that scar on her chin? When did she start smoking? Why does she stand far away from the microwave? Write for one hour. Invent a history for the character.

To Thine Own Self, Write the Bloody Truth

To be ourselves causes us to be exiled by many others, and yet to comply with what others want causes us to be exiled from ourselves.

—CLARISSA PINKOLA ESTES

When we are told that something is not to be spoken about, we understand this to mean that this something should not exist—should not, cannot, must not, does not exist. In that moment our reality and, consequently, our lives, are distorted; they become shameful and diminished. In some ways, we understand this to mean we should not exist. To protect ourselves, we too begin to speak only of the flat world where everything is safe, commonplace and agreeable, the very small world about which we can all have consensus. Soon we don't see the other worlds we once saw. For it is difficult to see what we are forbidden to name.

—DEENA METZGER

Truth waits for eyes unclouded by longing.

—Ram Dass

How moved do you have to get
to write about those who will be mad
when they read what you said if you dared
to say it or write it
Because your lungs will explode
if you don't.

—Frances Curtis, *Mired in a Literary Dilemma*

When I was growing up I was always looking for myself in the books I read. Thank god for Nancy Drew (a little too blond and a little too perky, but at least she was smarter and braver than Ned), and thank god for Dominique Francon (a little too mean and a little too tough, but at least she was strong and smart).

It was bad enough not to be able to relate to the stories in the literature I read as a student but to add to that, we could never write our own stories. We had to write research papers and essays on critical thinking and book reports where maybe—if the teacher liked you—you could sneak a piece of personal narrative in, like "The reason I enjoyed this book was the main character was funny like my grandfather."

Biographies of women like George Sand and Virginia Woolf and Margaret Mead weren't quite right either. Sure, it was nice to read about women who accomplished something (god knows I hadn't seen anything accomplished other than a whole neighborhood of women soaking their whites in Ivory Snow). And of course it was exciting that a few of these famous women were actual writers. But I needed more than the description of their madness and their failed marriages. I didn't know then what was missing, but I know now: I needed their inner lives. I needed the explanation for their behavior—what was going on inside them while they were drinking, sleeping, locked in one room. I needed to know about their loneliness, their fear, their pain. I needed their stories. And I needed their truth.

But too many women have gone mad not writing their personal narratives—their truth.

Women have experienced the same isolation, the same postpartum depression, the same "Sophie's Choice" kinds of horrors in our lives forever. Believing you are the only one who is having this nightmare is enough to make you think you are crazy. But suppose all the women who flipped out had had a best friend that they could have told *everything* to. And just suppose that when they confided to that best friend that there were times when they wanted to throw their newborn baby into the ocean, and there were times when they wished their husbands would die, and there were times when they could not get out of bed, that same best friend had said, "Yeah, I've had those moments, too." And just suppose that same friend had said, "Here's the name of the counselor I went to see." Or, "I'm coming over to give you a hug." Or, "There's this book you need to read." Or, "I bought you this journal."

Maybe all those women wouldn't have been healed, but at least they wouldn't have thought they were nuts. *And they wouldn't have thought they were alone.* You can bet that those ladies in the quilting-bee circles were not sitting around telling each other their incest stories.

We have not been telling the truth for a long time. And we have all paid dearly for the lies of omission.

One night after a big family dinner when the men (the husbands, the fathers, the guys) got up and went into the drawing room (well, we didn't have a drawing room, and they didn't smoke cigars, and there wasn't a football game on TV, but they did all disappear), seven of us found ourselves at the table talking about the first time we all had gotten our periods. Don't ask me how we began, but in the middle I remember knowing that this was extremely important and that it felt really joyous. I mean, there I was with my seventy-something mother and my seventy-something mother-in-law and my fifty-year-old sister and my thirty-eight-year-old cousin and my twenty-something-year-old niece and my brother-in-law's ten-year-old daughter. It was my mother who spoke first.

She said that my grandmother, who worked from eight in the morning to ten at night, had told her that "when she saw blood" she should just go to Mrs. Shapiro in 7B. And at the tender young age of eleven, my poor mother, terrified and convinced that she was dying of some rare disease, suddenly remembered the mentioning (not the preparing, mind you, but the mere mentioning) that blood might appear. She went to the neighbor's apartment, knocked on the door, and told Mrs. Shapiro that she was bleeding. Mrs. Shapiro promptly slapped her across the face and then in Yiddish cried, "Mazel tov!" (which means "good luck"). My little niece, a bit horrified herself, said, "Why did she slap you, Aunt Henny?" and my mother laughed and explained that she found out later it was a folk tradition to ward off evil spirits and at the same time to put color back in her face. We "tsk tsked," and someone said a sip of brandy and a hug would have done the same thing, and just think—you could have eliminated the emotional trauma.

Then my sister told her story. She was twelve and thought she was dying (do we have a recurring misconception?), and started screaming, "Nance, Nance!" I was eight and came running into the bathroom and, according to my sister, went right to the cabinet and brought down a whole bag of feminine supplies with the sales slip still in it, and taught her how to use the sanitary belt, all the while chastising her for forgetting "how Mommy had shown us all this last year." I hadn't remembered any of that, so it felt great hearing how my older sister had needed me. My mother-in-law said she remembered having to leave school because she was wearing a yellow dress, and once she got home (wondering if she was dying—have I heard this somewhere before?) never wanting to ever return to school again. We younger ones at the table were shocked when the two elders told us since there was no such thing as Modess or Tampax then, they had to use ripped wool rags. We all moaned and then my cousin Mirium told us how her mother had given her twelve white roses—one for each cycle of each month, how she had taken her out to lunch and gotten her a glass of champagne, and together they toasted "to becoming a woman." "Now, you're talking," someone said, and we all agreed. Then we looked at little ten-year-old Shaunan. We told her that if she ever had any questions we would be there to answer them, and that we hoped getting her period would be a wonderful rite of passage for her. We told her how much we would have loved to have heard these stories when we were growing up and that we hoped her experience would be a celebration instead of a humiliation.

Then, as I remember it, we got so excited thinking about how young girls would never be ashamed or feel that it was a "curse" again if they could have some association with it that was beautiful. It seemed the cultural shame was dissipating, and we could continue creating the shift in consciousness by bringing this open dialogue to a larger forum. "Let's make a movie!" we shouted in our best Judy Garland and Mickey Rooney voices. Before we knew it we were brainstorming about how we would get Kotex to sponsor it and the music would be all the songs from Blood on the Tracks.

Of course we never made the movie, but it was a magical night and the seven women at the table all still remember what it felt like to be able to tell their stories and have other women riveted to the details.

Why are our personal stories so powerful? Because they are true.

What is Truth? Someone said Truth is the gentle removal of denial, that when you are ready you can lift the veils that have kept you in darkness. There are no writing rules governing the time frame for such a removal, but the sooner you decide to grab the shovel, the quicker clarity rears its lovely head.

Why write the truth? (Come on boys and girls—you knew it wasn't a cliché for nothing.) The answer is, because there's nothing more powerful than the truth. Because writing the truth sometimes helps you face the truth. Because writing the truth is the beginning of living the truth. Because the truth shall set you free.

* * *

I didn't tell the truth for the first forty years of my life. I thought the reason I lied was that I thought I was protecting other people, but the truth is, it was to cover my own behind. I lied to my kids to get them to do what I needed them to do. I lied to my friends to get whatever it was that I needed. I lied to myself but I would never have known they were lies.

We live in a time where the truth is not really respected and is definitely not required. But the fact is that when truth gets compromised, everyone gets ripped off. Parents who lie to their kids about the fight they had last night ("No, we weren't fighting; that was the television") deprive them of role models of openness and honesty. The parents rationalize that it's for the kids' own protection (that protection thing again). But the kids know their parents had a fight, so what actually happens is that the parents have taught their children how to get around the truth. And as if that wasn't bad enough, they teach them that touchy topics are terrifying "no-no's."

Anyway, all the "spurtial" my-karma-ran-over-your-dogma reading got me thinking about my own bizarre approach to honesty, and I decided I wanted to start telling the truth. It might have helped if I had had an awareness buzzer around my neck, since manipulating to get what I wanted had become a habit. I wasn't a mean manipulator; I was a lovable manipulator, but if you weren't careful you'd give me your prized collection of porcelain dolls and thank me for taking them off your hands.

I had to learn how to take the chance of asking directly for what I wanted. Being direct and asking a fellow human for something, instead of tricking them into just handing it over? Asking and admitting I needed help? Excuse me? Damsel in distress kind of a thing? I'd rather lie. But, I started doing it anyway, and it got easier and easier. Now I get it and I clearly see the harm and know the danger of half-truths and withholding truths and white lies and beige lies and this-is-for-your-own-good lies.

This is what I realize: Being able to tell the truth makes being able to *write* the truth easier. And writing the truth is the beginning of healing the heart.

Now, when I talk about writing the truth, I'm talking about personal narratives. I'm not talking about fiction. I'm talking about not needing to have your readers think you're a good person, a hero, an honest upstanding citizen. I'm talking about writing from the heart with "the facts, ma'am—just the facts." This writing never has to see the light of day. This writing can be solely for your own purposes. Why waste your time lying to yourself yet again? Use the writing to get in there, go deeper, and find out what wasn't safe to find out before. Don't worry, nothing will come up that you're not ready for. And maybe the thing you're supposed to write about for the world has to start somewhere. So start somewhere. Just start. From the heart.

TRUTHFUL RELATIONSHIPS

Ram Dass talks about the many kinds of relationships there are. But he says the hardest one is the "yoga relationship." It's the relationship that dwells in truth. The deal is the two parties enter into a contract of sorts. Basically the agreement is something like this:

I will help you grow and you will help me grow. I won't need you to behave in a certain way to make my ego feel comfortable. And you will not make me behave in a way to satisfy your ego. I won't make you be anyone you're not. And I will love you for who you are. I will tell you the truth. I will tell it to you lovingly. I will tell it to you so you can hear me. I will tell it to you even though it will hurt you. I will tell it to you even though you probably won't like it. I will tell it to you because I love you that much. So when you are being an asshole I will tell you. In exchange for this I expect you to do the same for me.

The day I knew I wanted to have this kind of relationship with my husband I went bursting into the room and said, "I want to have a yoga relationship with you." He was reading about cold fusion in his bible, *Scientific American.*

He said, "I don't understand why I haven't heard anything more about the Patterson power cell."

I said, "Yoga means union."

He said, "There's enough deuterium in the seawater to power the energy needs of the human race for the next one hundred fifty million years."

I said, "It means we have to be completely truthful; we have to always tell each other the stuff that might hurt."

He said, "It would revolutionize energy. "

I said, "It would revolutionize our relationship."

He said, "Don't you think we already have one?"

I said, "One what?"

He said, "A yoga relationship."

I said, "Almost. You never really criticize me, though. In fact you've been defending me for years. And I thank you for it. I couldn't have heard anything critical for the first thirty years of our lives together. Your instincts were quite right. But now—"

He said, "But now you're ready to be torn apart?"

"No," I laughed, "but I could use some candor, some honesty."

"Okay," he said. Then he took a deep breath and said, "You're interrupting me. I was reading."

I turned around and said, "Thank you. I didn't think it would be that easy." And I left.

If you are not married to or with someone who loves you enough to tell you the truth, you can have a yoga relationship with writing, a writing life that is based in truth. It won't send you out of the room and it probably won't talk back about the virtues of deuterium.

In my writing workshop, people say they are afraid to write the truth, even in their own private journals. Daughters have found out their mothers smoke pot, mothers have found out their daughters aren't virgins, husbands have found out their wives are having afffairs, and siblings have found out they were adopted. Writing your truth is risky. But consider the alternative. Think about who you are writing for. Writing is where you can find out who and where you are. It's where you can truly celebrate *you.* It's where you can go with your fantasies, and no one can judge, no one can laugh, and no one can take them from you.

Maybe your family would like to continue thinking you are the perfect mother, the organized secretary, the keeper of the Scotch tape, and the for-splinters-only tweezers. Maybe the fact is that you hate having to know where the tweezers are, and you hate buying Scotch tape, and you have been holding yourself in for fifty years, waiting to go wild and be free. You have been dying to tell them you don't know where your little straw basket with all that stuff is and they can go looking for it, for all you care. How much longer do you want to deprive yourself of breaking out in order to protect others from who you really are? Maybe you can be true to yourself and still pull out their splinters.

Are you protecting yourself from the same truth they taught you wasn't good for you? Maybe you have to get a lock and key, maybe you have to tell them the truth, maybe you have to get a combination safe, but don't sacrifice your soul to keep the illusions in your family alive.

Things are not great in the world. Do you think it's because the air is polluted, or because the acid rain is killing the trees in the rain forest, or because cancer is on the increase, or because we found out priests weren't perfect, or because movies are violent?

We are hurting because we aren't real and because we don't live real. Because if we were living in truth, we wouldn't let any of those abuses in our world happen. We would understand the interconnectedness of ourselves with nature and with the planet and with our own souls and with each other.

What makes writing powerful is the universality of the truth. All of us want the same thing. We all want to be validated for who we are—not for who people want us to be. We all share the emotions of fear and pain and worry and sadness. Why, then, do we spend so much time pretending we're fine? When has that helped? A long time ago, maybe when your mother had too much on her mind, and your father came home tired, and your teacher just wanted you to sit still. But now the jig is up. You can't help your mother and your father and your teacher anymore by faking it and being the good girl. It's time to let the "bad" girl—the truthful one—out. Let her write her truth.

If you develop an honesty in your relationship with your words, you will begin to find the courage to stand up for more of what you believe in your life. The writing will be like a little rehearsal for when you decide to take the big stand. After you've written it you'll be surprised how much easier it will be to let these thoughts just roll off that courageous silver tongue of yours.

EXERCISES:

Write about a lie you told. Do not soften the circumstances. Be tough but gentle. Be tough in writing the truth, but be gentle on yourself. You were just being human. Do you think you're the only person who lied to get what you wanted?

Take a situation or a topic or an event that you haven't talked about honestly yet; something that is still stuck in your throat, like a tiny fishbone, small enough not to choke you to death but big enough to let you know it's still there.

Work on it in small amounts. Spend twenty minutes each day on it. Don't even reread it. Just write it. Truth is all you need to write. No gorgeous phrases, no sparkling syntax, just *truth.* Write until you've written the whole story.

Write about a lie that was told to you.

Write a diary entry from when you were preteen to teenaged. Write with your nondominant hand.

Women: Write about your first period. Include how you felt, what you were wearing, what you knew, who you told. Fill this piece with details.

Men: Write about your first encounter with menstruation. Use the same directions.

Are You There, Gut? It's Me, Margaret

How many times have you snapped your fingers, pounded on the table with disgust, and said, "Damn! I *knew* I should have brought that extra set of keys," or "I *knew* I should have gotten gas." If you *knew* so much, why didn't you pay attention? I'll tell you why. Because you didn't trust the little voice. And why didn't you trust that little voice? Because it's still so little you can roll over it like a golden retriever on a fresh manure mission.

Losing your keys and running out of gas are just the minor normal everyday disasters. What about the big ones where the little voice said, *Don't marry him*, or *Don't invite him in*, or *She's lying to you?* We make some of our gravest decisions without the most important part of the decison-making equation in place—our *feelings* about what's happening.

Remember, there is a triumvirate of *me, myself,* and *my gut* operating at all times. You need only to acknowledge its existence.

For a culture that has a million expressions for intuition (*hunch, sixth sense, gut, premonition*) it's funny how we slough it off to the esoteric. When we have a feeling about something and it actually happens, we are more comfortable echoing the theme from *The Twilight Zone* than giving our intuition credence.

Writers need to reconnect to their intuition, plug back into that place where there is only Truth.

Your intuition is your gut, your center, your chi, your power, your animal instinct, your dead and patient grandmother waiting for you to reawaken. It is your soul speaking. Your intuition will *never* lie to you. Clarissa Pinkola Estes in *Women Who Run with the Wolves* says, "Intuition is like a divining instrument . . . like a crystal which one can see with uncanny interior vision."

As writers, we need this uncanny interior vision. Our brains are so spoiled, so used to the power, while our poor little gut fights for one tiny shred of recognition. Why would we listen exclusively to our brains? Look who's in there: everyone who has ever said a bad thing to us, sitting right next to the formula for the isosceles triangle and under the dates of the Boer War. None of this information serves me when I have to make a personal decision. I don't trust my brain. It's stuffed with false information: don't go to Israel—it's dangerous (I went to Israel, had a remarkable time, and nothing dangerous happened); buy the cheapest house on the block—that way you can make the biggest profit when you sell it (we bought the most expensive house on a block that was decreasing in real estate value; we didn't care. We loved the house). When it comes to most of the important decisions in my life, I try to remember: The mind is a terrible thing to use.

As writers, we must go with our instant ideas, our immediate poetry, our "first thoughts," as Natalie Goldberg calls them. We cannot take the time to rethink, reconsider, reedit, restrain. It will sound like rewarmed oatmeal, twice-cooked spaghetti, watered-down coffee. Go with what comes up. Don't make time for your inner editor to happily announce, "They'll really think you're sick if you write *that*."

Recently I bumped into a former neighbor of mine. We hadn't seen each other since seventh grade. Her mother had been mentally ill, and everyone in the neighborhood knew it. My old friend and I got to talking about the "good old days," both of us agreeing how *ungood* they actually had been. She told me how, when she was four, three orderlies had burst into her house and put her mother in a straitjacket. She remembers watching from the window, crying as the ambulance pulled away, and asking her father where they were taking her mommy. Her father's tactless answer is still sitting on her chest. Matter-of-factly and without a hint of emotion, he had said, "Your mother is going on vacation." Imagine being four, and the adult in your life—the Reality Interpreter—just took his Swiss army knife and diced your perception into itty-bitty pieces. My friend doesn't remember how she felt at the time, but I'd put my money on the old knot in the stomach. How many of those lies do little kids have to hear before they stop trusting their inner voices? How many contradictions do kids need before they begin seeing the world through the cerebral lens of parental revisionist history, designer facts, and convenient fabrications to "spare" the child the pain of the truth? My old neighbor could have simply grown up with a distorted view of what vacations were, but I think the damage was far more crucial. She's on her fourth marriage. My bet is she stopped trusting other people and never trusts herself.

The father of a friend of mine committed suicide when my friend was three. His mother told him his father had gone on a wonderful trip and that he wouldn't be back for a long, long time. The mother remarried and never talked about the father again. My friend was an adult before he found out from cousins what had really happened. He's another one who doesn't remember how he felt when his mother lied to him, but the odds are that his little-boy stomach was in a knot (as in not feeling anymore).

There's a bloody trail of the walking wounded who either haven't felt a feeling since their slide through the birth canal, or who feel them but doubt them. These folks rely solely on their brains, keeping a tight grip on the intellectual order of life. Some of these people need to control *their* world, and sometimes *the* world. These people don't take heart; they take Rolaids.

What happened to you when the grown-ups in your life lied to you? If you were hurting, it was probably your intuition crying. Some people never had a chance to strengthen the connection between their tummies and the truth. And so, this connection, like all things that don't get enough attention and excercise, atrophied. The people who lied were the Intuition Murderers.

Writing can be the bellows for the dying embers of your intuition. Writing can breathe the life force back into you. The recovery might begin as a whisper. Or it might begin as a wail. But the writer won't miss it. Once you hear it, you'll realize you're in charge of the volume control.

So how do you begin to strengthen that fragile voice? You need to practice. Just like you would the flute or skating backwards. My friend

Priscilla studied with Barbara Brennan, the author of *Light Emerging*. The program includes an actual course called "Healing Intuition." As a college student, I would have killed to have gone to her school. I can picture my first meeting with my in-laws thirty years ago. It was bad enough that I wasn't wearing shoes or a bra. All they needed was for me to tell them I was going back to school to major in intuition, and they would have left town in the middle of the night with their son hidden in the trunk of their sensible car.

If you can't take the class formally, maybe you could design a course of your own. The syllabus would dictate that you leave your head with all your preconceptions and judgments and fears, and go directly to the blank page in your gut. Intuition is about trust. And you're the contractor you've hired to rebuild it.

I once had a student intern who brought his Saturday night angst to work with him every Monday morning. All of us in the office were in the middle of his romance novel. He kept asking us for advice, but when we would ask him how he *felt* about being in a relationship, how he *felt* about her, how he *felt* when he was with her, how he *felt* when he wasn't with her, he always had this confused look on his face. And then one time he very quietly asked, "How does anyone know how they feel about anything?" Both this young man's parents had been alcoholics. *Feeling* was a luxury he didn't think he could afford.

But feeling isn't a luxury; it's a necessity. It's your survival. It's your soul life. It's your truth. And without it, your art, your life, your writing will be generic—anybody's voice. With it, your work will be authentic, powerful—*your* voice.

Consider your intuition a muscle that needs to be exercised. So flex your gut, open your ears, pay attention to your belly. Your intuition is trying to guide you, and it's with you all the time.

EXERCISE:

Write about a time you felt one way and acted another. (When I give this exercise in my workshops, someone always says, "You mean my whole life?")

Be Here Now

LOST

Stand still. The trees ahead and bushes beside you
Are not lost. Wherever you are is called Here.
And you must treat it as a powerful stranger,
Must ask permission to know it and be known.
The forest breathes. Listen. It answers,
I have made this place around you,
If you leave it, you may come back again, saying Here.
No two trees are the same to Raven.
No two branches are the same to Wren.
If what a tree or a bush does is lost on you,
You are surely lost. Stand still. The forest knows
Where you are. You must let it find you.

—David Whyte, The Heart Aroused

I read Richard Alpert's (a.k.a. Baba Ram Dass) book *Be Here Now* ten years after everyone else had already put it on their tag-sale table. When it first came out, I was in another world, trying desperately to be a good suburban housewife. I had pressing issues, like whether to line my pantry shelves with red and white check oilcloth versus the more subtle baby blue. I spent my time worrying about whether I'd be invited to the New Year's Eve tennis party at "the club" and shopping for Marimekko fabric that I would then have made into pillows to match my Dansk couch.

I was so straight, I would have told Jesus to get a haircut.

But the book changed my life. It felt as if for the first time someone was finally telling me the truth. Ram Dass referred to life as a "journey of awakening." The minute I read those words, I was home. Mind you, I hadn't known I was away before. Lines like "The journey across the great ocean is a journey inward," and "The deeper you get in, the more you meet Truth," and "How do you ask your inner self for something? You are already it," felt like huge shafts of sunlight cutting through the middle of a dark, dark dream. I had been sleeping, and I hadn't even known it. I guess I had always felt that I was missing something, but had no language to describe it. I had lived with a longing that I constantly renamed. I longed to get married, then I got married. I longed to have children, then I had children. And then I longed to *do* something, *make* something, *be* something. The problem was, I had no idea what. So I longed and I languished and I filled my life with all sorts of unmeaningful stuff to distract myself from the longing. I read novels, I had my hair done, I had clothes altered, I tried new ways to make fondue, I had affairs. But I kept coming up empty.

It was 1967, and I had just gotten married. I'll never forget dragging my new husband to visit a woman I sort of knew who was making an animated film. Just the thought that there was someone in *my* town making an animated film was a thrill. I had to see how she was pulling off such a thing. So here she was, my age, photographing individual tears for a character in her movie. I was fascinated, watching her do her work. I was also insanely jealous, starving for the feeling she was feeling. There was an electricity around her, a sense of commitment, real importance, not *make-believe importance,* which I had already spent my life seeing and trying to imitate. My husband and I drove home in silence. When we walked in the door, I flung myself on the bed and sobbed. My poor, young, gentle husband had no idea what was going on. *I* had no idea what was going on. He stood, confused and helpless, asking, "What?" I remember my exact words. I said, "I want to make an animated film." I remember his exact words. He said, "Then do it." I was sure I had married an insensitive idiot. *Do it. Right. Sure. And while I'm at it, maybe I should sculpt a twin sister for the* David. It was easier to blame my husband, the town, the times, than to wake up.

I started buying every book that had Ram Dass's name on it. He didn't actually push god, but I could feel it coming. My relationship up until that point with any god concept was strictly limited to my verbal expressions like "Oh, my god" and "God forbid!" They were references, not reverences. Nobody was home behind the word "god."

The few times I let an actual godlike image creep into my consciousness, I'd picture the guy in all the paintings, the one who gave Moses the tablets. *He* was big and barefoot and stern and had absolutely nothing to do with me—unless of course, I needed something. Then there was always prayer. But that was another fraud, a droning mechanical plea. I never really expected anything, but at the same time I expected everything. Oh, I could go to temple and enjoy an occasional Bar Mitzvah. And I could go to the Passover seder and delight in singing *Deyenu* surounded by my loving family. But "God" had nothing to do with any of this. Now all of a sudden, the idea of God felt very natural.

I was suddenly being liberated from the guy in the white flowing robes, smiting and anointing, looking down and saying, "Nancy you're a bad girl; Nancy you're a good girl." Now I understood that God was my higher self, my truth, my connectedness to everyone and everything. God was nature. God was science. God was laughter, God was harmony. But most of all God was love. I remember thinking, "I can do this. I can do God!" Of course, while I was "being enlightened," I knew how my scientist husband felt about religion being the opiate of the people. But this wasn't religion; this was the real thing. No dues. No board meetings. No hierarchy. No power plays. No politics. Just in the heart from the heart, in the moment, unattached love-thy-neighbor—I mean, really love thy neighbor.

For some years it was a struggle, but that's because I kept thinking my husband was me. Once I stopped trying to make him feel what I was feeling, once I didn't need him to be who he wasn't, once he knew I wasn't running off to join any weird cult with orange silk turbans, and once he knew we didn't have to give up our worldly possessions (what with our extensive Marimekko collection and all), he became all ears. Since I was already all mouth, the best thing happened: We both headed for all heart.

Ram Dass was the teacher who became my alarm clock. He talked about not judging things as good or bad, about how judging keeps us from being in the moment. He must have written the book for me. If there was anyone who was president of the Judge Club, 'twas me. I judged weather: It was too muggy; it was too damp; it was too dry; it was too windy. I judged lighting: It was too dim; it was too bright; it was too cold; too blue; it needed more warmth, more amber, more subtlety, more diffusion. I judged vegetables: They were too limp; they were too crisp. I judged the restaurant they came from, the cook who cooked them, the pot that held them, the waiter who served them, the gardener who grew them, the ground that made room for them. I judged people by what their clothes were made of. Polyester was a big "don't" in my fabric "dos and don'ts." So if you weren't wearing 100 percent cotton, I pretty much wrote you off. It's frightening to think of the humans that I never had the opportunity of learning from and loving because I got my values from a fashion magazine. Oh, yes, I was a busy, busy judge.

Just after I read *Be Here Now* for the tenth time, I began my first discipline in my whole life. Every day, I ran 3.8 miles in the woods. And I was so smitten with the idea of *being here now* that for weeks I just kept repeating it to myself. The whole time I was running I kept saying, "Wow be here now!" Ram Dass understood that there is no other time but now, that being present fully is being without judgment. And being—just being—is exquisite. But right in the middle of one of my be-here-now thoughts I would suddenly think, *I wonder if there is cumin in that bean burrito thing I had at Eileen's.* Then I'd think, *Be here now. Yup. Winner. Be here now.* Then I'd think, *I'm always planning the future. If I'm not fantasizing about the future, I'm commiserating with myself over the past.*

Wow, I realized, I'm never *here.* I'm never *now.* I began to have a glimmer of an understanding of the meaning of "Life is what happens when you're busy making plans." I kept thinking, *From now on I'm gonna live in the NOW. I'm gonna live in the moment. I'm gonna be a moment mavin.*

Well, I just kept this inner dialogue going constantly, huffing and puffing, thinking and repeating; never seeing a tree, never tasting a breath, never feeling the air, when all of a sudden an acorn fell and bopped me in the head. I stopped in my tracks, looked up, and thought, *God is a stand-up comic*. And then I remembered that self-conscious moment of—God? Yeah, okay, God.

For the rest of the run, I tried to stay present, be in that place, breathe in that air, take in those words. But of course my untrained mind stubbornly kept returning to important stuff, like the recipe for Molly Katzen's sweet potato and black bean burrito.

The acorn incident was subtle, and one year before that I wouldn't have caught the humor of it. I would have stopped briefly, looked up, shrugged my busy little shoulders, and then gone back to the innane chatter in my busy little head.

Being here now is not so easy. Try sitting still, emptying your mind, and just *being*. If twenty "redo" conversations with your three closest friends, and eighteen new ways to redo the bedroom, and five different recipes for flan don't crowd in, all demanding equal time, then get thee to a Zen monastery at once. You're there. You're Zen. Your chakras are smiling. I, on the other hand, am still considering flan with skim milk and draping the window above the bed with handwoven Irish linen.

Some people learn to "be here now" as a survival skill. Julia Cameron in *The Artist's Way* says, "In times of pain, when the future is too terrifying to contemplate and the past too painful to remember, I have learned to pay attention to right now. The precise moment I was always in was the only safe place for me."

Another thing Ram Dass did was to give me what felt like a specially engraved invitation to let go of my expectations. He said, "Let go of how you think things should turn out." His actual expression was "Let go of the fruit of the action." He said you do what you do just because you do it. You don't do it because of the end result. You just do what you do. What a concept. Write without thinking about the acceptance call? Write without thinking about the made-for-TV movie, the public fawning, the seven-figure advance? Was this guy kidding?

If you can just do what you do and let go of all the *mishegoss* that keeps your pen from moving and your heart from opening and the words from coming, the experience of being present with your writing will be all that you'll need. The best writing time will be when you're not thinking about the bestseller, the fancy byline, the credit on the resume.

It was on Ram Dass's tapes that I heard him say to let go of the definitions of who you think you are, of where you're going, of where you've come from. He said we have a strong identification to our *somebodyness*: I'm a mother, so you have to be my child. I'm a boss, so you have to be the worker. I'm the shrink, so you have to be the patient. He says notice the roles, give them space, but don't think that's who you are.

One day recently, I took a break and drove down to Gay Head to my spot where I walk. As soon as I left my driveway, I began this agitating monologue in my head. *Look at all this traffic. Oh, my God. It's only March, and the energy has picked up. There's just not enough off-season anymore. Where can I go for my solitude? How can I get the winter I had last winter?* When all of a sudden I remembered a story Ram Dass told about being in the Borelli railway station in India. He had been meditating up in the mountains for months with his guru, and had to come down into one of the cities to update his visa. His train was about four days late. There he was with chickens and goats and children crying and the septic system backed up and the stench and the filth, and he was in bliss. He was truly in the moment. He had no mental models for how a railroad station was supposed to be.

My trip down to Gay Head, though not as colorful, was exactly that. As soon as I thought of the story of the Borelli railway station I let go of my expectations for what an off-season island road should be like in March. The sky was a breathtaking blue and the line in the road was a joyous yellow. And I could feel the buds on the bushes reaching for April. Here it was. The *be here now* of it all. So hard to do—so ridiculous not to do.

The moment doesn't disappoint. The moment always delivers. And then before the judge takes a vote on how we feel about that moment, there is another moment to be in and celebrate.

I feel as if I have found the Holy Grail. Of course it's one thing to know the Holy Grail exists; it's another to find it and still another to keep the sucker up on your mantelpiece.

Why it is so damned hard? The answer is, boys and girls—being in the moment means I have to stay awake. I can't tell you how tempting a little afternoon nap would be.

Many years ago one Mother's Day afternoon, I was scheduled to do a reading at a bookstore. That morning I woke up feeling like a fraud. *How can I stand up in front of people as if I were some kind of expert?* I hadn't written anything I was proud of, and I hadn't been on NPR in a while. I knew their introduction would be filled with glittering accolades and accomplishments that I didn't feel applied to me. I had a stomachache and a headache, and I was pacing in my office. How can I fake this? How do I perform when I feel so insecure and unprofessional? I stood in front of my bookcase and somehow my hand (I sometimes think the book actually jumped out at me) was reaching for a book my son had given me nine years before. It was one of those watercolory, swirly, rainbowy proverbs-and-wise-sayings books. The page fell open to the following: Right now you are exactly where you are supposed to be. I felt this calm come over me. It was okay to be lost. It was okay to feel insecure. It was okay to be in transition. In fact I was exactly where I was supposed to be. Being here now didn't always have to be Be here now if it's a good place. It meant being in the present with whatever the present presented.

We need to stay with the low moments. They feed the high ones. They add depth to your writing. They add depth to your soul. We are not wind-up toys with smiley faces. We are real beings with hard days and sad moments. That day, when I gave my talk, I began with the truth.

Living in the present connects you, rivets you to the moment. Writing in the present (tense) does the same thing. It gives readers a feeling of immediacy that connects them to that moment.

Since writing in the present is easier than living in the present, this exercise is foreplay for the real thing. Write it and then live it. Then remember that wherever you are is here and right now you are exactly where you are supposed to be.

EXERCISES:

1. Take any story you have written using the past tense. Then change all the verbs to the present tense.
2. Write a brand new piece in the past tense and then make the changes. Read them both out loud and see which you like best.
3. Start a piece with "I am standing at the refrigerator . . ."

Here's a part of a piece from one of my workshops. I told the class to write about a lie they told.

Here's the lie in the past tense:

My mother was on the bed, half awake. Somehow I knew intuitively that I was not yet practiced enough to lie to her when she was fully alert. Hopefully in this state I would catch her slightly off guard and my lie would pass.

I took another two steps into the room. I was almost at my mother's side now. She turned to me, still half asleep. I was wearing a schoolgirl's dress that exposed bruised knobby knees and pasty white legs. I hated the dress. I hated the knobby knees. I was hopeful that she couldn't see them tremble. I can't remember my face, but I cannot forget hers. An aquiline nose between two high cheekbones. Classic Greek sculpted features. Dark, passionate and piercing eyes. She was beautiful. She was a goddess. I was a five-year-old girl-child and I was about to lie to a goddess.

Now here is what it sounds like when she changed it to the present tense:

My mother is on the bed, half awake. Somehow I know intuitively that I am not yet practiced enough to lie to her when she is fully alert. Hopefully in this state I will catch her slightly off guard and my lie will pass.

I take another two steps into the room. I am almost at my mother's side now. She turns to me, still half asleep. I am wearing a schoolgirl's dress that exposes bruised knobby knees and pasty white legs. I hate the dress. I hate the knobby knees. I am hopeful that she cannot see them tremble. I cannot remember my face, but I cannot forget hers. An aquiline nose between two high cheekbones. Classic Greek sculpted features. Dark, passionate and piercing eyes. She is beautiful. She is a goddess. I am a five-year-old girl-child and I am about to lie to a goddess.

Experiment with some of your writing. Read the pieces out loud and switch tenses back and forth.

Who Can Write?

This is the shortest chapter in the book.

Because the answer is, *anyone.*

Who can write with no dangling participles?

Who can write about the anatomy of the elbow?

Who can write a grant proposal?

Those are different questions. But who can write a personal narrative, a novel, a story, a play?

The golden answer is *anyone.* (And that means YOU!)

Feel, Deal, and Heal

Once you've brought the bulldozers in and they've pushed down the cement wall around your heart—the one that you spent all those years building—you might not be able to rush to your desk and start writing your autobiography. You might need to do a bit-o'-healing first. Nothing like wholeness for bringing greatness into the world. There are a million self-help books for healing everything from having too much phlegm to integrating multiple personalities. I can only give a few hints that helped me and that have helped people in my workshops.

Three winters ago it snowed about every three days. The white was brilliant; the air was clean; the sky was clear. My husband and I spent more time walking outdoors than we ever had. I was happier than I had ever been. I had spent so many years in this marriage waiting for him to "get it," and now I was finally realizing there was no "it"—there was no right, there was no wrong. There was only different. We had completely opposite takes on the world, and for the first time I was seeing his point of view, honoring it, learning from it, laughing at my having been blind to it. And he was doing the same. In fact, we were learning that our differences were the most interesting part of our marriage.

One day we were in the middle of a laugh that took us down, bent over, almost peeing in our pants, when all of a sudden, out of my husband's peripheral vision he must have seen or felt someone approaching. He stood bolt upright and stopped laughing. A man walked by, not paying much attention to our antics. My first reaction was anger. How could my husband have let a stranger interrupt the ecstasy we were having? But then I remembered his perspective; his reserved, shy—big-displays-of-public-anything discomfort. I went from my small selfish reaction to his. I said (not as a personal criticism, but a universal commentary on the way things are), "Fun Police!" We laughed even harder. "What a strange world we live in," I continued. "Why do we feel compelled to straighten up and hide our joy when a stranger walks by? Instead, why doesn't *he* feel compelled to double over in laughter?"

SHOOT YOUR TELEVISION

One day after consciously not having watched television for a while, I turned on the vicious little box and the weatherman came on and said in a most apologetic way, "Sorry folks. Here comes another horrible storm. This is the worst winter since *blah, blah, blah*." I sat there, furious, thinking, *How can this guy tell me how I'm supposed to feel about the weather?*

How can he tell me how I'm supposed to perceive precipitation? He's deciding for me what snowfall means?

The fact is that his negative, "winter-sucks" attitude is actually how I had lived most of my life, but it so happened that at this particular moment in my own personal journey, I was in the middle of a rebirth. For the first time, I wasn't cold in winter. For the first time, I was connecting with Nature and understanding my place in her. And here was this guy, this authority figure in a suit and a resonant bass voice, trying to take that away from me. I could feel myself almost slipping into his perspective: slipping in the slush, on the black ice—oh, the danger, the inconvenience, the bitter cold. But I hadn't been having a bitter experience; I was having a sweet one. And this guy was stealing it. No, I was *letting* him have it. He was in my house because *I had let him in.*

I grabbed the remote and nuked him. But then I thought about it and wondered, *What else are they telling me about how I should be feeling?* After my own little informal study, I found that the answer was, *everything*!

I reminded myself that the networks' main goal was to sell product. In order for them to exist, they had to have *me* buy what they were selling. Their message was relentless: Happiness is a new Buick, or a new dinette set, or a new breakfast cereal. Nothing I already owned or had inside of me would come close to what a little shop-till-I-drop would do. They promised that consuming, buying, shopping, spending, charging, no-money-downing would make me happy. But they never mentioned how temporary the thrill of a new window treatment was. I couldn't help but notice how I had never heard them advertise a walk in the woods. Could it be because there's no profit in tree appreciation?

My friend Peter, a psychiatrist, says when patients are depressed he asks them what they do to relax. He is disheartened at how many of them say they watch television. He explains to them that the body needs to rest, to recharge, and that they may *think* they're relaxing because they're zoning out, but the fact is that every organ of their body is being assaulted for every second the television is on. Even if it's a decent program, his patients are *engaged.* But that the body needs to *dis*engage. So if you want to do some healing, turn off the TV, tune out the world of commerce, and drop in to your hungry heart.

My friend Elliot has been meeting twice a year with ten other doctor friends for over a decade. They spend those weekends sharing their lives. One of the psychiatrists described Prozac this way; The problem with Prozac is that it's so good. He said since he has been using it for his own depression, he has come to realize that he had taken his hand out of the fire too soon. Writing your story is a way of keeping your hand in the fire just a little bit longer. It's hard to burn when it's so easy not to have to. But try writing the gory details of your pain first. Then if it's unbearable, do what you have to do.

CRY

Several years ago I was diagnosed with a hiatal hernia. It's not life-threatening, and I hesitate to complain, in view of what some of my fellow beings have had to contend with. But even though I knew my life wasn't going to end, I still felt unbearable pain almost every day for almost three years. It felt as if a truck were on my chest, and there was severe burning in my esophagus. I went to every doctor, every specialist, every alternative healer I could find. The Westerners gave me barium milkshakes and stuck things down my throat. They pumped me with Valium, Atavan, Gaviscon. If it was on the heartburn shelf, they gave it to me.

I had acupuncture, I went to chiropractors, I took homeopathic remedies. All the alternative stuff helped considerably, but the tenacious hernia aways returned. Then I read Louise Hay's book, *Healing Your Own Life*, where she lists ailments, possible reasons why we get them, and affirmations to heal them.

I looked up *hernia* in Hay and it said, "ruptured relationships" and "incorrect creative expression." I closed the book and harrumphed. My relationships were rock sure, I thought, and just because I wasn't writing, I was still making homemade valentines, which certainly qualified as "correct" creative expression.

A year later, a friend and I were looking up *bladder* because she was always getting bladder infections. It said, "Anxiety, holding on to old ideas. Fear of letting go and being 'pissed off.' " She couldn't believe how close it was to the truth. We looked up another friend's lower back pain. It said, "holding onto anger." We gave each other that knowing nod. I decided to look up *hernia* again. My life had been in such a mess the first time I checked out the book, I wouldn't have recognized a cure if it crept up my esophageal and sang, "I'll be down to getcha in a taxi, honey."

This time, with a little distance from the whole thing, I was able to see the obvious connections. That's when I decided I wanted to have something to do with my own healing. At the same time, I started doing yoga and going for massage. The minute the therapist touched me, I had permission to release all the tension of those trying times. And I started sobbing. I wailed and I cried and I sobbed and I wailed. After three weeks of yoga and sobbing, I was completely healthy.

I had always been a crier, but that was when I began my serious sobbing campaign.

Once, when I was in the middle of crying, my husband said, "Well, Nance, when is this going to end?" And between sniffles and the temptation to laugh, I said, "You want an exact date?" We were in the car on the way to the beach. I was bringing *Women Who Run With the Wolves* by Clarissa Pinkola Estes (not exactly beach reading). When we got there, I opened to *Battle Scars: Membership in the Scar Clan.* The first line I read was "Tears are a river that takes you somewhere." It was as if Clarissa herself had come out from behind the pages and said, "Look, you have been working so hard at this. Why not sit back and have yourself a big bowl of wisdom." These are more of her brilliant words:

> *"Weeping creates a river around the*
> *boat that carries your soul life. Tears*
> *lift your boat off the rocks, off dry ground,*
> *carrying it downriver to someplace new,*
> *someplace better. . . . A woman's crying*
> *has been considered quite dangerous,*
> *for it loosens the locks and bolts on the*
> *secrets she bears. For most women these*
> *secret stories are embedded,*
> *not like jewels in a crown, but like black*
> *gravel under the skin of the soul."*

All most of us want is for our boat to be lifted off dry ground to someplace new, someplace better. All most of us really want is to be loved, to be validated, to be held, to be heard. Maybe our costumes are different, maybe our interests are different, maybe our tortures were different. But the human condition is always the same. We want recognition.

We want to be able to be who we are. We want to be real. An occasional hug shouldn't be such a radical concept.

Sometimes you want to heal so badly that the clues will pile up outside your door waiting for you to take one baby step toward the handle. Other times it's harder to pick up the messages. Whatever work you choose to do to go inside and tackle the demons is up to you. The goal is to go back home to where the heart is.

Staying numb might be more attractive than bleeding from every pore. You need to know that a willingness to feel your feelings doesn't mean you have to define yourself by them. You can get depressed, but you don't have to be a depressed person.

When my younger son was diagnosed with MS, I cried and sobbed and beat my chest. I couldn't find relief in my husband's arms or in the blue-green ocean that had always made the world okay for me. I walked around in a cloud of black flies buzzing and biting at my open wound. One night we were invited to two parties. One was where everyone knew about our tragedy and the other one was where people didn't even know who we were. We went to the party where we would be strangers. We ended up having the first good time in a year and a half. We laughed and we joked and we sang on the way home in the car. And that is when it hit me. If we had gone where we were known and loved, people would have come up to us with their kind concern and their sympathy and we would have stayed comfortable in our tragic role of parents of a child who has been struck down. We had begun to define ourselves that way. By going to a place where we could transcend the pain—reinvent ourselves—we were able to be free of the miserable events we had been living with.

This is not to say that we don't continue to feel the bone sadness of the situation. But it means that now there is a place for it, a balance. It is not us; it is *part* of us. By getting some distance, we were able to inhale clear air for the first time in months. I remember almost feeling guilty singing on the way home that night (*How dare you be free of pain for a minute!*). It was the balance we had needed. And the timing was right for the balance. That first year, I clearly needed to carry the full burning pain around every day. I didn't know it, but that's what grieving is. After that night of relief, I realized then it was time for me to move into a new phase, that of being a survivor—but not a hardened survivor—of one of life's larger curve balls.

Lots of comics have turned their childhood pain into humor. They become the voice for all of us who've suffered. Hanging on to old stuff that no longer serves (as mine wasn't serving me) was putting a crimp in my life, so of course it was affecting my writing. It's easy to buy into the myth that your alcohol is your brilliant prose, or that your cynicism helps you access emotionally complex characters, or that your miserableness is your creativity.

It's hard to do the "psychic dig." But the payoff is that if we can heal our lives, and with that healing bring clarity and wholeness to our art—and to the world—we are ahead of the game. We get to love what we do, and do what we love. Maybe comedians grow quite the healthy funny bone during their hard times, but just because they get healthy doesn't mean they have to get serious. They may lose their desire to make people laugh, but there's no proof that they also have to lose their ability.

I have a responsibility to my fellow humans to feel. I know plenty of folks who feel. They are only too happy to tell you how they feel. *I am so miserable. I am so unhappy. It hurts so much.* There's no map for *how long* or *how to*, but dealing with your pain comes right before healing, and healing is the reward. So why do all the work—why eat all your vegetables (even the brussel sprouts) and not get the chocolate pudding with the whipped cream?

Why not start to feel it, and why not continue to heal it, why not sit down and write it, and—what the heck—why not get it out there and sell it? You could be the comic who gets to laugh all the way to the ATM machine. Or the writer who gets to walk in the woods without spending a dime.

EXERCISE:

Which story in your life do you want to feel on a new level? Which story keeps resurfacing for years and wants to be written? In a workshop where I gave the exercise, "The last time I saw him . . . ," a woman whose brother had been murdered forty years before said she had wanted to write this all her life. She had never made sense of it, and never allowed herself the anger and the relief. There had been too much guilt. Her first line was "The last time I saw him, I was identifying his body in the morgue." She wrote the beginning for what she considers the most important story of her life. She was ready to look at how every event after his death was shaped by that moment.

Write *The last time I saw . . .*

Write only the first page and leave it. Go back later, and don't censor anything. Begin adding to it. Be gentle with yourself. No one has to read this but you. Each day for two weeks, add to the story. Keep everything you write. Don't throw away any of it. Save everything; you'll need it for later. You may need distance to hear some of your best lines. Keep writing from your heart. Keep coming back to "I."

Nothing Comes from Nothing

Come, Come, whoever you are,
Wanderer, worshipper, lover of leaving—it doesn't matter.
Ours is not a caravan of despair.
Come, even if you have broken your vow a hundred times.
Come, come again, come.

—JALAL AL-DIN RUMI

"I have no discipline. How can I get myself to write (paint, walk, practice the piano) on a regular basis?"

This is the collective plea I hear in my workshop over and over. It's as if we all expect to wake up one morning with the discipline gene.

I hate to tell ya, but there's no easy answer. If you want discipline you have to keep slowly adding, building, and staying with it until one day, doing it feels better than not doing it. It's like doing sit-ups.

I was the original "there is too a free lunch" person. To me, discipline was the *D*-word, and a dirtier word had nary been spoken. But after years of thinking someone else would finish my story, write my book, clean my refrigerator, build my arm muscles, I finally realized that discipline was the only way I could go. I had always thought freedom was not combing my hair and saying "fuck" in front of grown-ups. But it turned out that discipline is freedom.

Discipline is a dedication to your truth. It's discipline that gets me out of my head, into my heart, and back to work. I had always thought work was a dirty word. It was to be avoided at all costs. Who knew how delicious it was to work hard and stand back and delight in your own efforts?

So, if discipline is one of your ten plagues, read Scott Peck's blockbuster *The Road Less Traveled.* In it, he talks about delayed gratification (a phrase I used to think was an oxymoron). He tells the story of a thirty-year-old financial analyst he was treating in therapy for her lifelong problem with procrastination. He asked her if she liked cake. She said yes. He asked her what part of the cake she liked best and she told him the frosting. Then he asked her which part of the cake she ate first. And she said the frosting, of course.

As a therapist, he was able to help her to see how her cake-eating habits were the same as her work habits. She realized that on any given day she would devote her first hour to the part of the project she liked, and for six hours she would drag through the more mundane, boring stuff. He told her if she were willing to force herself to do the unpleasant thing in the first hour, she would then be free to enjoy the other six. He told her that it seemed to him that one hour of pain followed by six hours of pleasure was preferable to one hour of pleasure followed by six of pain. That did it. She saw his logic, and finally solved her procrastination problem.

But we all know that intelligence has nothing to do with it. Some of the smartest people who've had heart attacks still go to McDonald's for lunch.

I once heard an interview with a writer whose early superstar success had completely immobilized her. They were interviewing her because after thirty years she had just made a stunning comeback. When they asked her why she started writing again, she said because the pain from *not* writing got even worse than the pain from trying to write.

I am married to a cheerleader, a Mr. Stick-to-Everything-Until-You-Have-It-Conquered. He has never been aware of his own remarkable tenacity, but I witnessed it during the years he studied Suzuki violin with our sons. He would practice with them, and often after I would go to sleep, he would stay up for three more hours practicing by himself. Many times in the middle of the night, he would burst into our bedroom and wake me with: "Nance, I made a breakthrough! Listen to this!" And the nine notes he had been haltingly squeaking would now be a smooth mini-symphony—a personal concerto for one at three-thirty in the morning played by a guy who understood the religion of practice.

If someone were to ask you if you'd rather be miserable or happy, you would probably say happy. It's that direct a choice. Once you have tasted it, you will never let it go. You may slip into hibernation for a few seasons, but I guarantee that all you'll need is a kick in the bee-hind and a paintbrush, pen, flute—whichever your tool—in your hand. The discipline I'm talking about is not inflicted—it's *desired.*

If discipline is one of the things that you think might be holding you back, maybe a redefinition on your part would help. Think about the times you were successful at things that took commitment and perseverance. Maybe because you loved doing them, you didn't realize they were work.

Discipline can be defined as something you do consistently that is hard. Just because you get high from it, doesn't mean it doesn't get points. Just like eating the frosting first, we want the reward first. In work that requires discipline, the beginning is always the hardest part. But if you stick to it—you can make it from *hard work/tedious drudgery* to *hard work/euphoric frosting.*

Think about something you worked on, loved, and completed. How did you work? What was your process? Did you wake up early in the mornings and work while everyone else slept, or did you steal your time late into the night? Did you wait till the last minute to do it, as you used to with exams, or did you plot and plan and plod along methodically, getting a little done each day?

The point is, you got it done. The thing to know is that everyone does it differently. There is no right or wrong way to honor your work. The temptation to compare yourself to anyone else—particularly those whom you admire—will lodge itself in your "should house." You *should* get up at five in the morning if you really want to finish that novel, you *should* write every day for two hours if you ever want to call yourself a writer, you *should* make an outline and keep it posted next to your computer. Who are these people telling *you* how to do *your* work? Tell them what Ram Dass says: "Don't should on me!"

When I heard that John Updike worked from eight to noon and then someone brought him his lunch and then he went back to work from one to six, it threw me into the "I'm-not-a-real-writer" whine. I told my husband what I had heard. "But you're not John Updike," he said. "Exactly!" I snapped. "And you write about *your* life and that means *you* have to live it." "Right," I said, unconvinced. "You *are* disciplined," he continued. "You're just not miserable, so you think you're not disciplined." I breathed a big, "Whew!" and, momentarily convinced, went for a walk in the woods.

Some people need to fill and recharge more than others, but their work gets done. Others don't recharge till they pass the project in. Everyone's got a different approach. And everyone's got an opinion about your approach. Luckily my husband's opinion had my best interests at heart. You really are the only one who can tell you if you're slacking or working. I heard somewhere that Thomas Wentworth Higginson, one of Emily Dickinson's editors, told her she wasn't disciplined. Please.

The next thing you might want to do to make this discipline thing happen is to make your work space beautiful. Make it so you want to be there. We talked earlier about making altars, lighting candles, bringing flowers. All of these will help you want to go there. Any creative contrivance you can use to get you into the workspace will do.

I have one friend who goes to her computer every night after work and writes a nasty letter to her ex-husband, which she never mails. She prints it, rips it up, and then looks at a photograph of her two beautiful babies and begins her work on her novel.

I know someone whose teenage son used to play a game called Dark Castle with her on her computer. It was one of the few things during his stormy adolescence that they were able to do together without fighting. Now he's away at college halfway around the world, and each morning she plays one game of Dark Castle right before she writes.

One woman blushingly confided to the group on the last day of class that she has a whole sexual ritual she does before she writes. She said, "This is going to sound really strange, but once I get this sexual energy out of my body, my creativity just flows."

Some people meditate before they write; some use the writing practice as the meditation itself. But as Gypsy Rose Lee says, "Ya gotta have a gimmick." What do you care if it's a trick, as long as it does the trick?

Just remember: Writers write. And that the reward for having discipline is greater than any hot fudge sundae you ever tasted or velvet dress you ever imagined.

When I talk to my painter friend Lori after she has slogged her way through a week of not making any headway (positive she should throw in the towel, if not the whole linen closet), she always says the same thing: "Maybe I don't have it anymore. Maybe I'm just not cutting-edge." And I always say the same thing back to her: "Haven't I heard this before? And what, may I be so bold as to ask, is 'cutting-edge'?" We always laugh, but I can hear the doubt. Then she calls me back three days later and I can hear that she's made the breakthrough. This happens over and over and over again. And it happens because we have experienced the freedom that comes from discipline. But these are just words, and until you have experienced the high from what my jewelry designer friend Jude calls "Krazy-gluing yourself to the seat," they are empty and feel like your father is lecturing you. I'm not lecturing and I'm not your father, but I want you to have this because it's the domino of joy. Discipline affects every part of your life.

I also know it's hard to believe in yourself and keep going back to the drawing board if you have no outside proof that you're good. But "good" is a judgment that others make, and "bad" is what you feel if you believe them. This is not about good or bad. This is about "following your bliss." Do you think Joseph Campbell was talking about shopping for cashmere? Your bliss is what you're supposed to be doing—the thing you're meant to do, the thing that nourishes you the most, the thing that harmonizes your inside truth with your outside life, the bringing together of who you are with what you love doing. So don't wait for the reviews. Siskel and Ebert are never going to come to opening night in your bedroom.

You just have to want it.

FOR THE YOUNG WHO WANT TO

Marge Piercy

Talent is what they say
you have after the novel
is published and favorably
reviewed. Beforehand what
you have is a tedious
delusion, a hobby like knitting.

Work is what you have done
after the play is produced

and the audience claps.
Before that friends keep asking
when you are planning to go
out and get a job.

Genius is what they know you
had after the third volume
of remarkable poems. Earlier,
they accuse you of withdrawing,
ask why you don't have a baby,
call you a bum.
The reason people with M.F.A.'s
take workshops with fancy names
when all they can really
learn is a few techniques,
typing instructions and some-
body else's mannerisms

is that every artist lacks
a license to hang on the wall
like your optician, your vet
proving you may be a clumsy sadist
whose fillings fall into the stew—
but you're certified a dentist.

The real writer is one
who really writes. Talent
is an invention like phlogiston
after the fact of fire.
Work is its own cure. You have to
like it better than being loved.

For those of you who have stuck to something, anything that required your fierce devotion, remember the baby steps you had to take before you were a full-fledged marathoner? In the beginning, maybe it was the hardest thing you'd ever done: getting up at the crack of dawn, forcing yourself out of a warm bed into the cold, dark morning. It took forever to push through the initial misery. Then as the joy of accomplishment, the thrill of completing something started to seep in, it got less miserable. It was still horrible, but now there was a reason. Each morning you would forget the reason, but some dim memory would start to knock at your brain and you'd be able to do it—one more time—and one more time—and one more time. And pretty soon it became impossible for you to go a day not doing it.

Once you have discipline, you can let your own insides dictate your rhythms. Maybe there will be a day when you don't want to run, paint, write. Gently give yourself permission to skip whenever you need to skip. This is the balance between hard work and knowing that sleeping in, holding a cup of hot tea, and staring at nothing is part of that hard work. It's the recharging part, it's the balance part, it's the honoring yourself part.

Discipline makes something come from something.

So the next time you are tempted to say, "I have no discipline," change the words to, "I choose to be happy. I choose to give myself this gift." Then, if you still can't sit down and do your work, go back and read Rumi again. There will always be another Monday morning.

EXERCISES:

1. Write your definition of discipline in a sentence or two.

2. Describe in three sentences your process.

3. Write a short piece on something you accomplished that made you proud.

4. Write a letter to yourself telling yourself about something you wish you were doing that you're not.

5. Make a list of three things you stuck to that were hard. Did any of these give you pleasure either during or after the work was completed?

Process, Not Product

When I lived in Connecticut, I was a regular on Colin McEnroe's radio talk show on WTIC in Hartford. At first I was a wreck. I would be shaking and stuttering and interrupting, trying desperately to sound clever and funny and intelligent. Half the time I was so busy thinking of what *I* was going to say next, I couldn't hear what Colin or his callers were saying. The few times I did take the chance to jump in, I found myself repeating the nonsequiturs my father used to serve up with Sunday brunch: "I think it's colder in the winter than in the country," "What's the difference between an orange," and "Do you walk to school or take your lunch?" They were funny when I was eleven.

I would be mortified as Colin ran with whatever malapropism I had fed him, obviously unaffected by my incoherent babblings. Our rhythms were different, and because I was so nervous, my timing was always off.

Once, a caller asked me what I thought about Duvalier, the Haitian president, going to a psychiatrist. I hadn't read a newspaper in months and had no idea what the world was doing. Instead of admitting I didn't have a clue, or even quipping something comedic, I just stammered and blushed and tried to recover my equilibrium. Still, my amateur enthusiasm must have been appealing to Colin because he kept inviting me back. And so it was that I became one of Colin McEnroe's straight men (or women). And even though I had hoped I would be his perfect match, and even though I would slink out of the studio praying the receptionists wouldn't realize that I was the jerk whose inanities had just been broadcast, the thrill of being on the air was greater than the shame.

After about fifteen guest appearances, I bumped into a woman I knew. She said, "I always hear you on Colin's show." Comments like those aren't really questions or compliments, so it's hard to respond. I said, "Isn't he brilliant?" (which I believed). She said, "Yes, he is very quick." And then she added, "But why do you let him make such a fool of you?" I was stunned. I spent the next few days wondering what it was that kept me going back for more. I hated the thought that my hunger for recognition was that strong, but I had to admit it was. I almost called the producer of the show to tell him I wouldn't be on anymore, when I thought, *I love doing this and I want to get it right.* I knew deep down that I could if I kept trying. I asked my husband if he thought I had gotten any better. My champion said he thought I had been great to begin with, and that I was still great. I laughed and said, "I'm never going to ask you when I want the truth, but you sure are wonderful when I don't."

I decided to go on the show once more, but this time I would go prepared with something spectacular, something so engaging, something that I knew so well that I wouldn't sound hesitant or uncomfortable. And no matter what curveball came my way, I'd be able to handle it like a professional. I chose the following story:

> *There are two Milton Friedmans. One was Reagan's financial advisor and the other is a writer. The writer received a phone call one day. The caller on the other end of the line said, "I represent several churches in California and we have amassed quite a fortune. We would like advice as to how to invest it." Milton Friedman the writer knew of course that it was a case of mistaken identity, but decided to play with the guy a bit. So he said in all seriousness, "Have you considered donating it to the poor?" The caller snapped back, "Is this the REAL Milton Friedman?" to which Milton Friedman replied, "Is this the REAL church?"*

Well, I practiced this story in the bathroom, in my car, in the mirror, with my friends, until I had the thing down. I was too embarrassed to bring notes because, aside from wanting to impress the whole radio-listening audience with my storytelling talents, I also wanted to impress Colin. So, notecard-less and seemingly fortified, I arrived at the studio and announced on the air that I had a great story to tell. There was the usual banter: the news, some ads; Colin made me read the weather, and finally he asked for my story. By this time I had stirred up a good batch of nervousness and I couldn't remember that Milton Friedman's first name was Milton. My mind was racing through the alphabet. Al? Bill? David. David Friedman? My face must have been contorted with anxiety, because Colin said something like "Aronie, what is it, a bedtime story? Do we have to wait for dusk or something? I already know *Goodnight Moon.*" I was rattled, but "Milton" came to me just in the nick of time. So I continued, but there was something about not having any human faces present that made me think that I was droning on forever. I thought I was further along in the story than I was, and I began to rush to wrap it up. Instead of saying, "Is this the real Milton Friedman?" which sets up the whole thing, I went right to "Is this the real church?" It was a joke with a premature punch line. I died. This story was less than two minutes long, and I couldn't pull it off.

Then Colin jumped in and said, "Ladies and gentleman, this was not a good story. Should we just ban Aronie from the program altogether? Why don't you give us a call and let us know how you feel about the return of Nancy Aronie? 1-800-278-9000." Then there was an ad and I was apologizing to Colin and the lights were blinking and the calls were coming in. The next thing I remember was being in my car listening. One woman said, "I don't know why you have her on in the first place. She's not that funny." The next guy said, "I think you should give her another chance." Three more people called and said things like, "I never understand what she's talking about, anyway."

When I got back to my office, there was a message from my mother. It said, "Hi, honey. Call me." My mother is the consummate nourisher, and at that point I needed consummate nourishing, so I called her back immediately. The first thing she said was, "You should never go on his show again." I gulped and said, "Why not?" She said, "Well, honey, because, um, he humiliates you. And if you do go on, you have to start reading the newspaper again." And then her voice kind of dropped and she said gently, "And I just don't think you're that good at it."

I sat there trying to figure out why this was such a big deal to me. And why each individual hair on my arm was bristling and why the insults from the listeners were less painful than my mother's *You should never go on that show again.* And then it hit me. "Mom," I said, "I grew up in a house without process. I never saw anyone get better at anything. I didn't even know you *could* get better at anything. I never saw anyone practice anything. I didn't even know what practice was. If you weren't good at something right away, there was no point doing it at all."

Then I started crying. "I wanted to get good at this. I don't know why. I guess I wanted to conquer my fear of being in front of a microphone live on the air. And I know I can't get better in my kitchen with the safety of my cabinets that can't talk back. So I have to make my mistakes in public." I continued, "This has nothing to do with you. This is about my being embarrassed, and you just happened to be at the wrong place at the wrong time." "No," she said, "I'm the one who was wrong. I just want you to know how much I admire you. I'm so proud to even know you, much less be your mother." We gave each other a kiss and we hung up.

And then I sat there, miserable. After three days of being convinced I was the largest loser in women's history, Colin called and asked me to be on the show that next Monday. Maybe they don't count votes in radio. I said yes, a resounding yes. And that's when I decided to take a closer look at my non-relationship with process. It wasn't the first time I ever connected my feelings—about my lack of discipline, my reticence to try new things, my struggle with trying to stick to things—and the meaning of process. But it was the first time I was ready to look at it and not look away.

Process was what my husband was always in the middle of. He was practicing juggling three balls, and he was in the *process* of learning four. He knew how to play a simple waltz on his violin; now he was in the *process* of learning a more complicated piece.

Process was a foreign language to me. I was attracted to it. I knew I wanted more, but I wanted it immediately and I wanted it easily, the very antithesis of process. With process, there's no such thing as instant or easy. This was tough, although now I understand that there is work that is worth tough. I had to want something badly enough, and I had to see process up close and personal to begin to get it. "Anything worth doing is worth doing poorly" is at the bottom rung of process.

Process is not something you can teach, but it is something you can learn. Process is not the part we hear about. Product is up on the marquee, but process is the blood, sweat, and tears that put your name up there.

The problem is, I never fantasized about the process; I fantasized about opening night. What will I wear? How will I do my hair? Who will come? What will the reviews be like? I never had the fantasy of sitting at my desk working. I never thought, *Hmmm, my chair will be green and the light in the room will be warm and the music I'll put on when I'm writing will be Miles Davis.*

Process is intangible and unteachable. It happens all by itself, but you have to start somewhere. It's sort of like the Magic Eye, those three-dimensional art games that have me frustrated from the minute someone whips one out. I am sitting there trying so hard to "get it" without working at it. Or I am working too hard, without the letting go. Process is about balance.

Process doesn't have to come from some high-minded, God-inspired epiphany. It can come from as simple a place as *I want to do this.* It can come from as low as the ego crying for its long overdue due.

I would be the wrong one to diminish the role of ego, since it's been a helluva motivator for me. It didn't let me sleep until there was applause.

It didn't let me rest until I bought a computer. My friend Jude says the ego is like a pair of jumper cables; they get you started, but then you have to do something on your own to keep the charge.

So I learned to harness ego energy. I let it rear its jealous head when I read Anna Quindlen's *One True Thing,* I let it nag me when I saw Wendy Wasserstein's *The Heidi Chronicles,* and I let it beat me up good whenever there is something out that I should have written. I let it shame me into sitting down and giving myself a chance.

It's only when I stay in that place of envy and woulda-coulda-shoulda that I create a hell realm for myself. There is no key, no release, except my acknowledging that this is about my fear—fear of starting out not great. How can I write garbage?

But were Flannery O'Connor's first lines, first attempts, first drafts brilliant? I doubt it.

I know myself. And I know it's only when my ego gets lodged between my heart and my work that it presents a problem. But if I acknowledge that ego has been the origin, the genesis, the instigator, then I thank the little maniac and move on.

The main thing I always have to remember is that my ego doesn't have my best interests at heart. It wants the Oscar. But it doesn't care a bit about my soul.

EXERCISE:

Write about your relationship to process. Write about one thing you have or would like to get better at.

Make a contract with yourself that you will begin this practice now. Write the contract as a piece. It doesn't have to be notarized, so you don't have to leave the house.

I____

hereby agree to learn______________________________

____

____

Signature____________________________________

Maybe We Should Talk a Little Bit About Writing

On the first day of the workshop, I tell my students that I don't think anyone can *teach* writing. Teachers can guide, nudge, give examples, inspire, show some mechanics, teach a few rules (then encourage that they be broken), point out a few organizational skills. But basically, writing is about accessing the gold mine sitting inside each and every one of you. It's about understanding that your story is worth telling and being willing and courageous enough to write it. The root word of *courage* is *heart* in French.

And so in my workshop, I don't teach. I allow. Gerry Storrow, a poet and former student of mine, says the ideal teacher is the midwife for words that want to get out. I like that, because I believe *everyone* can write. But what babies want to be born into harsh glaring light, hostile hands pulling and wielding sharp scalpels? Creativity needs gentle, compassionate coaching.

Lary Bloom, a writer and also my first editor says, "You can teach that writing is a religious experience. You can help the writer reconstruct what it was that moved them about their own experience, but you can't teach a person to be Hemingway." So maybe a good beginning is accepting the fact that you're not going to be Hemingway. Great! You'll live longer and you won't have to waste your time shooting cougars and cleaning your gun. So, right away, you made a good choice.

The phrase *topic sentence* is never uttered in my class, and words like *dangling* and *participle* and *clutter* are never spoken, either. Yet exquisite writing comes out of every workshop. The only job I do, the only promise I make, the sole objective that I have is to guarantee safety. Once, on the phone, a man was registering for my workshop and I gave him my whole rap about how I don't really teach writing but I make it safe. He said, "Why? Do you live in a bad neighborhood?" I laughed, but the sad fact is that we are so unaware when we aren't safe and how necessary safety is to the psyche that we sometimes put ourselves in psychic danger (like reading a new poem to an old roommate, the one whose only comment on any of your stuff was to always immediately point out your flagrant abuse of the subjunctive). And then we wonder why we can't write. When we feel safe, we don't judge, we don't criticize, and we don't humiliate each other. That doesn't mean we don't give constructive suggestions and honest feedback. But because it's safe, people can hear. This safe environment (this womb of your own) is about giving nourishment and honoring each individual voice and listening to each other.

I know this works because every week, ten people arrive in my workshop tentative and terrified, and four short days later, ten people leave empowered and ecstatic. Every week I see ten miracles occur. People write pieces that they are shocked came out of them. I have learned that this is not surprising; this is what happens when people feel safe. So in a group setting, the participants become the teachers for each other.

I have come to understand that writers need help undoing the red marks that scarred their tender creative tissue, tissue that developed a hardness, a callousness that keeps the writing cold and the reader out. But safety and unconditional love are the salves that soften those scars.

As writers, you must learn how to translate your emotional experience onto paper. And that means melting your fear, using your fear, exploring uncharted terrain, experimenting with the unknown, going as far to the edge as you can, allowing your imagination to run free and naked over the hills and through the trenches, marching right past the mean old troll (your censor). Remember that it's impossible to melt fear when there's a big block of ice surrounding it. The block of ice is often right in our own backyard. So melt it, or move.

I asked my photographer friend, Diana, if she thinks photography can be taught—that is, beyond the mechanics. We were walking up a hill toward someone's beach house. It was off-season, and the summer furniture had been left outdoors. There were seven beautiful wooden chairs in a semicircle. She was starting to remove two of the chairs to take a shot when she said, "My teacher says, 'Expect nothing, that if you come upon seven chairs, you have to know that two of them need to go.' " And I said,

"That's funny. I tell my students just the opposite. I tell them to expect everything. And just as I said that, a hawk flew low and close. We found ourselves standing at the top of a hill, a hawk in our direct line of vision with a background of three juniper trees, all arranged as if Diana had moved them into perfect photographic position. It was as if the god of the arts had said, "Okay, I'll give these two an example of why both of them are right." That reinforced what I have realized a hundred times before but always forget—that there are no rules when it comes to creating. It's the balance of "expect nothing" and "expect everything" that reminds me to bring what I need to the work, and to trust that the universe will provide the rest.

This idea of being a partner with the universe is not just comforting, it's inspiring. I know I am not alone, and when I trust that support will kick in just in time, it always does.

Buddhists say you must have the perfect balance of wisdom and compassion. If you have too much wisdom then you are unfeeling, cold, like marble. If you have too much compassion, you become too sentimental. Balance your life, they advise, and balance will follow in your work. What a nice goal. The goal doesn't have to include a completion date; let's not say, "I want to be balanced and enlightened by June twenty-second for the summer solstice party." You do what you can, when you can.

So the following few chapters hold some writing hints. I'm not teaching, I'm hinting.

EXERCISE:

Find something that consists of interdependent elements (like the yin yang symbol) and write a page on an element's relationship to the things it depends on.

Point of View

R*ashomon* is the 1951 film directed by Akira Kurosawa and based on two stories by Akutagawa Ryunosuke. It is the story of the same violent crime shown four different times from the four differing points of view and varying degrees of self-interest of the three participants and the one witness.

For years, I have struggled with the fact that my husband and I have two very different perspectives. However, lately we keep starting out far away from each other and ending up at exactly the same place.

The Fibonacci series is a phenomenon where each number is the sum of the two that precede it. Fibonacci, a medieval mathematician, discovered that this odd feature was found in nature, such as in the way sunflower florets are arranged, the way the mollusk shell grows, or the way daisy petals are arranged. My husband and I were walking one day, shortly after we had learned about this. I said, "I don't understand why you're not thrilled with the Fibonacci thing." He seemed to take it in his stride. I said, "I mean, don't you think it's amazing that math is so obviously in nature?"

And he said, "No, I'm not surprised. Math is the *explanation* for nature. If there were no nature, there would be no math. Math is the language of nature."

And there it was. I said, "Wow, that's exactly what I think about god, that nature is the language of god. If there were no god, there would be no nature or the other way around. I'm not really attached to which comes first in the sentence."

It turns out, neither is he.

The more we have these dialogues, the more I realize that we are coming together to meet in the center where god and science are one. Who would've thought? It was a matter of respecting each other's perspectives. It only took thirty years. (I don't like to rush into anything, especially personal growth.)

Our perspectives change, and as writers, we need to move out of the tininess of our worlds and into all the possibilities. Being rigid and stuck keeps your writing rigid and stuck. There are many ways to skin a mango.

My sister and I went to visit the house we had spent seven of our youngest years in. The woman living there let us amble freely through the rooms. We couldn't get over how small everything was. The yard, which had seemed like a park, was a nine-by-twelve dirt carpet with worn spots and one lone lilac bush. The bedroom we had shared when we both had measles, where our mother had pulled down the dark green shades, barely had room for the two twin beds we slept in. The kitchen where we mixed make-believe magic potions to keep the scary big neighborhood boys away was tiny, and the pantry where we hid when they banged on the door and yelled, "We know you kikes are in there!" had only enough room for a six- and a ten-year-old to crouch and wait till their parents came home from work. We marveled that we had never told our mother how scared we always were, and how relieved we always felt when we heard their car pull into the smaller-than-we-remembered-it driveway.

Our perspective has changed. The big house is now small but the fear is still big.

In the early seventies, I saw the movie *My Dinner With Andre*. The whole movie is a dialogue between two old friends who haven't seen each other for some time. Andre is an eccentric aging hippie who is searching for the meaning of life, and Wally is the practical guy who stays back in New York, trying to write plays and pay the rent. When I first saw the movie I thought Andre was nuts, a kook, so far out he almost frightened me. I identified with hardworking, schlumpy Wally. A few years ago, I rented the movie and watched in utter amazement, because I had shifted my allegiance completely to Andre. In fact, I had become Andre, and Wally just looked like a whiner who was still afraid to have his adventure.

Just as in *Rashomon*, there are as many perspectives as there are witnesses. There's a story about a painting of a huge gray cloud in a large blue sky with a bunch of other clouds nearby. But when the framer goes to frame it, he says, "I'm sorry, I don't have a frame big enough for this painting," so he folds over the canvas. Now if you see this painting hanging on the wall, you would think it is just a painting of solid gray. Don't let a framer limit your perspective. Frames can be made in any size.

Besides, some things should never be framed.

EXERCISE:

Think about the places you have stayed stuck. Think about the limitations you have put on seeing from other points of view.

Write about a situation where your perspective has completely changed. Don't be hard on yourself. Just write where you were then, and where you are now. Write with no judgment. Write from the heart.

Write an argument between two people. Let one of the characters be you. Then write the same argument as if you were the other character.

Write a paragraph on each of the following:

In a romantic couple, the man should be taller than the woman.

You should arrive at an event to which you have been invited twenty mintues late.

Kids are kids and don't have anything to teach adults.

People on welfare are takers.

If You Can Talk It You Can Write It

Every one of you is a storyteller. Your ancestors sat around a campfire or a sweat lodge or a table and recorded their histories by telling their stories.

Now you tell them. You tell stories with beginnings and middles and endings. You are clear, you are articulate, you are funny, your tale has dramatic tension. You have perfect timing, your language is real, your attention to detail is impeccable.

You burst in the door of your house and pick up the phone and call your best friend. If someone were taping the conversation (without your knowing it), you would be amazed at how terrific a communicator you are.

You begin. You don't begin with, "Carole? Is that you? Is this Carole?" No, you begin with, "You're not going to believe what happened!"

I'm sitting at the light. I'm fiddling around with the radio—you know how at the bottom of Mountain Road you lose WPOP? So I pop in James Taylor's Live *and I'm singing "Shower the people you love with love and show them theee way that you fee—eel" at the top of my lungs.*

I sense something, but I keep singing. I look over, and who is sitting in his red Jeep Cherokee? (You pause, you wait a beat. You scream.) *Kevin-fucking-Lee. And he looks unbelievable. His hair is blonder, his beard is fuller, and his eyes are greener than they have ever been. Of course, every day this week my hair has looked great. But today—not only am I having a bad hair day, but I woke up with dark black circles under my eyes and a brand-spanking-new zit in the middle of my forehead. He is sitting there staring straight ahead as if he's wearing some kind of a neck brace that won't allow him to swivel. I know he knows it's me. Finally I turn up the volume and scream, "Fancy meeting you here!" and then—you're not going to believe this—he looks over and he's got tears in his eyes. I have never in the seven years of knowing him seen tears in his eyes. I turn everything off. . . . I say, "What's goin' on?" You ready for this?*

(You pause because you know the importance of the dramatic pause, plus you are emotionally involved with this story.) *His baby brother died. He tells me this at the fucking light. Timmy. Remember Timmy? Drowned in their hot tub. His mother had a breakdown. She's at the Institute. And he had to come home and take care of the other kids. I wanted to jump right out of the car right there and hold him in my arms. But just as my heart was melting, I remembered that he was the bastard who twisted my wrist so badly that I have a permanent bruise. Thank God, at that exact second, the light changed.*

Now, admittedly, this was not great prose, but it was conversational. It was intimate. It had a beginning, a middle, and an end. I cared about the people. And I cared about the outcome. It was a pretty good story.

Now, suppose this same person had to write this story for a school assignment. How do you think it would begin? I'll show you.

Having driven past the intersection of Albany Avenue and Mountain Road at the base of Avon Mountain in my automobile, my awareness, as I approached the red light, was filled with some unexplainable trepidation. My hair, which I had washed meticulously each night this week, was disheveled and unattractive, whereas on other days it had looked rather acceptable. In addition to this, my eyes, usually alert and youthful, were ringed with dark circles. Et cetera, et cetera, et cetera.

Suddenly your passion and your breathlessness and your immediacy have disappeared. Gone is the electricity, and in its stead is a stilted, uninteresting, forced beginning of a story I don't (and you don't) care about. You have lost your voice.

But somehow, in school, we thought this is what writers should write like. After all, your subjects and your verbs matched, your adverbs were modifying the verbs they should be modifying, your margins were indented properly. With all those things to think about, the creative aspect, the real voice, might have gotten buried under the avalanche of the prospect of the dreaded grade. You thought if you could just sound intelligent and like a "writer," you could get at least a B. And you probably did.

This problem begins as soon as your writing is for someone else. Here, it is for the teacher. If it were for a short story contest, the censor might have kicked in and said, "You can't say that four letter word. You won't win. Besides, what will people think of you if you use that word?" Are you still writing for your teacher's approval? For your father's approval? Isn't he the guy who spent much of his time reminding you that

"Anything you try will turn out like everything else you've ever tried—a mess"? Or your mother, who has always told you, "All that silly poetry is just a waste of time"?

It doesn't matter which enemy resides in your head, there is always a critic, always a censor to tell you what's *wrong* with your writing—never a cheerleader jumping up and down with your special initials on her sweater saying, "You go, girl!"

EXERCISE:

Write about something that happened to you that you told someone about but have never written down (preferably fairly recently). It doesn't have to be earth-shattering. It can be remarkably unremarkable. But it happened to you, and it involved some emotional response from you. Write it as if you are telling it to your friend on the phone or across the table. Don't cross out and start over. If, when you're telling this story, you say *um uh,* write *um uh.* If you pause, just write huge dashes like this————Just write, and stop when you're done. You can read it over once and see if there are a few minor changes you want to make, but no ripping up of paper and no ripping out of hair.

Leave the story for a month. Go back to it and change the names. Then go back again and change the ending. Add anything that wants to be included. Let the characters talk more. Have them think out loud. (*Why did I tell that woman on the bus I had an abortion? What's the matter with me? Why do I have to tell everyone everything?*)

Give some background so the reader has more information. (*I couldn't tell Jamie. She never would have understood. I couldn't tell my parents. They never would have forgiven me. I had to tell someone. A complete stranger can't tell me not to come home for Christmas.*)

Now you've got the beginning of a story. Stick to it and give it time. It will unfold just like real life, bit by bit. Tragedy by tragedy, joy by joy.

When you are finished, read the story out loud. Read it into a mirror in the bathroom. Or read it sitting on your bed. But listen to the sound of it. You will know what to take out and what to add. You will know if the skirt was purple but the sound of purple was too harsh. You will know to change it to lavender. You will know if the stranger needs to become a friend. You will find out if the story is about the father or the daughter or the mother or the stranger. Historical truth only works when it is about the emotional truth. The little facts like what color, what food, what country, might have to be changed. Take your poetic license and take a drive down the highway of your imagination.

Before you are so quick to crumple up your paper and chuck it into the wastebasket, read it aloud. Writing gets better in the reading. Call a friend who is safe. Tell him or her you don't want criticism, you don't want compliments. You just want a sounding board so you can hear your own words. You are listening for the good parts. Probably there are one or two great lines, or just words. When you are finished reading, thank your friend and hang up and underline what you liked. If you found nothing, keep it anyway. Don't throw it away. You might have been too hard on yourself that night.

But read everything out loud, and listen with a gentle ear. Listen for sound, listen for vulnerability, listen for realness. Don't listen with your judging closed mind; listen with your wide-open heart.

The Interior Voice

In real life, our minds are like meteors with thoughts crashing and bouncing off each other, fragmenting and sending little bits of mental particles to the far reaches of our imaginations and back before our mouths have emitted one word.

We are constantly bombarded with stimuli that the brain has to process. There are hundreds of split-second associations we have to make and still be able to function in a car, in a meeting, in a conversation.

When you see a person who has hurt you, there is no technology designed that could process all that is taking place, especially the emotional component. What you say to her and what is going on inside of your head are often two very different things.

You, as the writer, have to be inside everyone's head and heart simultaneously. This takes knowing who these people are, their histories, their foibles, their stories. This is how you can write precisely how they would react in any given set of circumstances.

One thing that makes writing rich is when you can give us a few of the layers at once. In real life, we get only what the speaker wants to give us, and we can only speculate and wonder about the subtext. In real life, wondering is part of the deal, but in writing, you can keep your reader informed, using multidimensions.

The following vignette is an example of interior racing thoughts and spoken controlled dialogue:

The Scene: a supermarket, aisle 5

Two women recognize each other at opposite ends of the aisle.

WOMAN ONE: Hi, Sally. How are you? *If she comes up to me and starts her whole litany of questions, I will throw up on her head.* (Woman Two comes closer.) You cut your hair. *Oh my God, she's even uglier than she was. This is a face that begs for long hair.*

WOMAN TWO: How're the kids? Did Dougie get into early admissions at Brown? *Get ready for a half hour on Dougie, the most perfect child in North America. Please let him not have gotten in.*

WOMAN ONE: *If she thinks I'm going to give her the satisfaction of his rejection, she's got another thought coming.* I think he's gonna take the soccer scholarship Penn State offered him.

WOMAN TWO: *I knew he wouldn't get into Brown.* I didn't even know he played soccer!

WOMAN ONE: *Of course she knows he plays soccer.* (Touches woman two's face.) It frames your face. You look ten years younger, I swear.

* * *

Here you see how what we say has very little to do with the full-length play that is being performed in our heads. A writer knows this and writes about everything he or she sees, making it very funny or terribly tragic. But the thing to remember is that it is always human, and it is always real.

EXERCISE:

Write an interior dialogue of your own.

Details, Details: Graphic Details

The written word has no visual accompaniment. It must be so clear that the reader gets as much information as possible to make the story come alive. That's why details were born.

Anyone packs a suitcase. Anyone packs two T-shirts, one dress, one pair of jeans, one bathing suit, one pair of shoes, one pair of sneaks. The writer packs the white Donna Karan turtleneck and the navy blue rayon mesh long-sleeve Polo number, the faded-to-perfection *501 Levi's* that you "traded" (stole from) Billy Martinelli when you slept over and found they fit perfectly, the Norma Kamali jade green and black pinstripe bikini with the gold buttons up the side, the black espadrilles with the silver grosgrain ribbons, and the pink high-top Reeboks.

Generalizations are boring; rich descriptions are compelling.

E. B. White told new writers, "Don't write about Man, write about *a* man."

Henri Troyat said, "No detail must be neglected in art, for a button half undone may explain a whole side of a person's character. It is absolutely essential to mention that button. But it has to be described in terms of the person's inner life. . . . Tolstoy characterizes old Korchagin by his 'bull's neck,' Mazlenikov by his 'white, fat fist,' Katyusha Mazlova by 'her eyes as dark as wet black currents' and her slight squint, Missy by 'her tapered thumbnail.' "

I have had students say, "But I have nothing exceptional that happens to me. What can I write about? Everything I see is ordinary." I say, Memorize where you are this minute. Look at your surroundings. Ordinary can be exceptional. The reader will recognize ordinary if it's specifically ordinary. A half-dead light pink African violet sits on the glass-top table with smears of Windex that look like early-morning beach sand. Who didn't water the plant and who tried to clean this table? There's a whole story here. All you have to do is take the details and move them to the left—or to the right. Your roommate in college got a phone call that her mother had been killed in a car accident. You have never forgotten the look of horror on her face when she dropped the phone and it dangled like a mini vinyl slinky. Now you've got a character and her dying plant and her dead mother. Go write. You don't need the whole story; it will unravel itself. But you must start and you must describe the room, the phone, the furniture, the lighting, the floor where Hurricane Hugo left its mark, rust stains that reminded you of the Van Gogh sunflower print in your first apartment in San Diego.

Trust that you have all this within you. Because you do. You have lived, and you have experienced. It's in there, and if you are willing to sit with it, give space to it, drop into your heart with it, it will come.

EXERCISE:

In about 350 words, describe a character, someone you know well, to a blind person who has to go find this person. Overdo the details. Then, in approximately the same number of words, see if you can capture the essence of this person with very little description. You're in charge of what you want to see.

Just for the Smell of It

Writing from the heart is not just about writing from the heart. It's also about writing from and *for* all the senses. Readers want to feel, they want to taste, they want to smell.

The minute I smell disinfectant mixed with bacon grease I am immediately fourteen again, working in New Hampshire at a summer resort. To get the job, I had lied about my age and my experience, but whenever I smell that smell, it is not *my* lie I remember. It is his.

He was nineteen, and already in college. He wore blue oxford button-downs and penny loafers. He knew all the words to "Earth Angel." And he wrote funny poems to me on the thin white hotel stationery. When I smell chlorine near cooked pork, the whole *Doctor Zhivago* love story replays in my head, and instead of enjoying my diner breakfast I remember my broken heart.

I loved every part of my receptionist's job that summer. After all, I was a teenager, and everyone thought I was a grown-up. My love and I would meet on our break in the huge pantry among shelves that held giant cans of SS Pierce peaches and gourmet olives and pimiento mix. The smell of the cleaning agent they used to wash the kitchen floor remains as strong in my memory as the smell of the gardenia corsage he gave me, which is still pressed into my parents' *Encyclopaedia Britannica* under *M* for *Marty*.

That's how the smell of a summer growing up marinated in Clorox and innocence can, all these years later, still have a life of its own.

This is what one woman from Manhattan wrote in a ten-minute writing exercise in class:

> *Every time I smell cigars, I think of my Grandpa "Tiger" and how much I loved him and the way he used to sit in his easy chair in the living room of his three-story house in Maplewood, New Jersey, watching baseball on TV. Grandpa always had a stogie perched cockeyed in his mouth—one eye squinting from the force of his cheek pushing towards the sky. On Sunday mornings, he would wake up with the sun and in his Bloomie's nightshirt would tiptoe quietly downstairs to make coffee and read the paper and prepare the ritual bagels and lox brunch for the rest of the family. By the time I woke up, Grandpa was always dressed, splashed lightly with Paco Rabanne cologne, and fitted with a big, fat, brown stogie. Once, when he wasn't looking, I snatched his cigar from the ashtray and took a puff from the soggy end. Even though it tasted bitter and stale (thank God I knew* not *to inhale), I loved chewing on the end, and I loved even more practicing perfect hand positions and blowing smoke out in thin streams, just like Olivia Newton-John in* Grease.

EXERCISE:

With a partner, choose four strong-smelling objects. First, inhale the odor from one of the objects. Really take in the odor. With your partner, present the items one at a time to each other. Then start writing associations. Make a list as fast as you can. Don't think—just write. Do the list of associations with each one.

ONION:
tears
strong
translucent
layers
glazed
fried
rings
soup

Now take any one of the associations and begin writing. Don't change. Stay with your first choice. Go anywhere with it. Remember, you can't be wrong. Both of you write for fifteen minutes. After you have done all four, you can then read them to each other.

Smelly suggestions include baby powder, burnt toast, nail polish remover, cat piss, pine cones, ripe banana, fresh popcorn, coconut oil, lavender soap, dirty sneakers, mildewed sponge, baked apple, wet dog, chocolate cake.

Part II

The thing that I didn't see in the fairy tales or in the suburbs was that everyone has a gift. James Hillman says we are born with it. He calls it the acorn theory. He believes just like the mighty oak is encoded in the acorn, so our individual genius is present in each one of us at birth. He believes that depression and frustration isn't about what our mothers did to us, but rather it's about not finding and wresting that gift right out of ourselves.

I didn't ever call myself "depressed" (it was such a Jules Feiffer cartoon word), but in retrospect, looking at what I did with my time and my heart, I'd have to say, Yup, I was always circling, never centered, never focused, always going off half-empty. Once in a while, I would see a glimpse of the "writing mountain" and all of a sudden I would feel, *There it is. That's what I want.* But who knew about climbing? I thought other people could climb—rich people, pretty people, smart people, jock and jockette people.

Every once in a while I'd get a reminder that this mountain thing was there for me, that it was waiting, and that it was climbable.

All I had to do was get some hiking shoes. But in those days, hiking wasn't for everybody—just professionals. So I'd write a poem and lose it somewhere in the house or read it to someone before I was finished or just not write it at all.

Every so often, though, there'd be a clear day, and on those days, I could see farther than before. But it was so hard to keep the mountain in focus.

When I went into therapy with a Jungian dream analyst, together we created a "hearth for my fire," she said. My energy was all over the place. "We need to contain it," she said. It was an image I could imagine.

We worked for four years, and little by little I started writing. One day, years before I owned a computer, I raced in and proudly told her I had written a story that I actually loved. She said, "Where is it?" I said, "Oh, it's in my car." She said, "Do you have another copy of it in safe-keeping?" I said no. She said, "Is your car locked?" I said no. Then she just sat and looked at me. And all of a sudden I got it. I jumped up, yelling, "Excuse me," as I tumbled down her steps.

And then I locked my car and protected my story.

I had finally gotten my hiking boots, and now I could begin the long ascent up the mountain. I would at last begin to honor my gift.

Getting a Ph.D. in Creativity

Art is not a vocation, but an attitude.

—Rollo May

Creativity is the true expression of your self. If you've got a self, you've got creativity.

Artists wear strange clothing and sleep much too late in the mornings.

Artists: we love 'em and we hate 'em. On the one hand we call them kooks; on the other hand, we look to them for our reflection. We ask them to tell us who we are. But we get nervous when their answers hit too close to home. We have a secret admiration for their irreverence, because down deep we would be irreverent, too, if we weren't such 'fraidy cats. So we let them do it for us. It's easy to write them off, particularly when their hair is blue. They don't play by the rules, and where *are* their Ph.D.s?

When I was growing up, if someone described someone else as "creative," it was almost as an apology, an explanation as to why they were different. "Oh, he's creative." It was said the same way you'd say an ugly baby was so "alert."

But then I'd also hear people say, almost reverently, "I have this friend, she's so creative . . . " as though somehow their friend was tapped by the goddess of artistic sensibilities, and the rest of us had been left for the kosher caterer who needed another mound of chopped liver. I thought some people were born to be artists, and other people were born to be plumbers. I guess I lived in a culture that was confused about creativity. Artists were either put down and ignored, or elevated on pedestals that were way too high for normal breathing. Of course, breathing didn't really matter that much, because most of the artists on the pedestals were dead white men. I never knew an actual living artist back then, and the way art was taught, I never connected it with real people. When it came to the creative arts, I just memorized the names, the dates, and the pieces, and hoped I'd get at least a B+ on the quiz. That was art.

Required courses never included music, theater or art—those were *electives*. Required courses trained the brain; electives served the soul. And there was no value for the nourishment of the soul. Who even talked about such a thing as *the soul*?

It took me until recently to understand that being creative doesn't involve making a thing that hangs in a place, that being creative means staying very close to my heart, to my instinct, to my desire, to my truth, to my soul. Kids do it all the time. They don't take the day off and think, *Maybe I'll do something creative today.* Everything they do is creative. They don't say, "I think I'll do a little finger painting." They are *compelled* to do finger painting. They wouldn't think of *not* doing finger painting. The only thing that would stop them is Playdough. I had bought into the idea that to be creative meant having an exclusive membership in a secret elitist club—the Creativity Club. I thought you couldn't belong unless you had a degree from the Rhode Island School of Design; unless you went for drawing lessons at the fancy museum downtown; unless the teacher chose your picture to hang on the classroom wall.

My mother is a creative person, although no one would call her an artist. She takes precious care in the way she puts flowers in a vase. She chooses thoughtfully which container to use. She picks each stem with concentrated attention. She cuts their lengths so they're not all the same. She moves things around and tries different spots on the table before she is happy with where she ultimately places the arrangement. When she makes someone dinner, she garnishes the plate with a sprig of fresh green parsley and a big red strawberry or a slice of bright yellow lemon and a trio of black olives. Then she stands back and sighs a sigh of satisfaction, knowing she has just created beauty. I see what it gives her, and I know what it gives me—this small act, this ordinary action. I know how I feel when I take the time to emulate her—rather than serving my usual huge amount of food with no attention to detail, or using the *plop-the-flowers-in-a-jar-of-water-there-I-didn't-kill-them* approach.

I often ask people about creativity. Do you think everyone has it? Where does it come from? How do you explain a Mozart? Can you be creative and not produce an object of art? Can you fake it?

When I asked my friend, Niki, if she thought an accountant could be creative, she said an accountant has to believe that two plus two equals four. But an artist has to know that there is always the potential for two plus two to equal five.

I asked my seventeen-year-old friend Gina if she thought everyone was creative, and she said yes. "So what do you think happens to teenagers?" I asked. "They're afraid," she answered. I asked her if she thought it took courage to be creative. "That's it," she said. "It takes too much courage. Because it's really who you are." "Aah," I said. We had hit on something:

YOUR CREATIVITY IS REALLY WHO YOU ARE.

I've asked lots of artists the same question. And what I hear is that they didn't wake up one morning and go, "Yippee, I think I'll be a starving artist." For most of them, they just couldn't help themselves. It was what they did. It was who they were.

My friend Margo tells me how her husband, a fisherman, goes out to sea and chooses to fish in the middle of the rip where all the tides coming from all different directions meet. There is a terrible turmoil and mixing and pounding and beating of the waves. In the middle of this chaos, he does his most successful fishing. Margo is an illustrator, and she says it is the same for her when she goes to paint. Her energy and inspiration come from a place of tension.

I've heard artists say that they have to get out of their own way, that the work they are most happy with is the stuff that balances their unconscious with their conscious minds. I hear artists say that when they are working, they have no idea what they are thinking or what the thing is about. Their mental connection is gone and in its stead is a trust that whatever is supposed to come through them will come through them. That in its purest form it's not planned, not contrived; that even though sometimes it feels like it originates from the mind, at some point the mind gives over and the creation begins.

Someone's explanation of Mozart was that it was almost as if the music was pouring through him and he was writing it down as fast as he could, and that if someone had said, "Mozart, you're incredible," he would have said, "If I see him, I'll tell him."

My brother-in-law Ron, who is sixty-three and has been a working artist his whole life, says he has to surrender to his first thought.

That's how I used to play Trivial Pursuit: The first answer that popped into my head was usually right. But then the doubt would set in and the discussions would ensue and I would get a little shaky and I would compromise with the loudest voice on the team, and then I would let go of what I had thought in the first place. Often my first thought had been the right answer.

When Ron was designing one of the gorgeous tables I own and he came up with the first thought and the censor didn't have the chance to say, "No one is going to buy a pink three-legged table with a red cherry apron," he must have sat down and begun to work.

Thomas Moore talks about creativity and living the creative life as being more about the *way* you do things—not the things that you create. You are both the painter and the tree you are painting. So maybe our current definition of creativity is too narrow and leaves too many people out.

My mother would probably be the first to go if there were a "creativity cop."

You can be an artist, whether it takes the form of sticking flowers into a vase or having babies and loving them as divine or throwing pots and loving them or loving yourself, being yourself and sharing yourself.

If you decide creativity is more about attitude than about God-given talent that only the few receive and the rest pay admission for, then you will have to develop an acute awareness of your own creativity. This attitude switch from "I have to get this thing wrapped before my kid goes to this stupid birthday party" to "Let's see . . . I've got a supermarket brown bag, I've got the red velvet ribbon that came on the box of valentine candy, and I've got the silver sparkles left over from Christmas" becomes a declaration of independence, a chance to make a joyous choice. It doesn't take more time, more money, a better marriage, a nicer car. Easy? Nope. Worth thinking about? Yup.

Comparing what makes a thing more creative than another thing doesn't make any sense to me. Of course a perfectly performed Chopin mazurka compared to a lovingly made tuna fish sandwich with a smiley face on the lunch bag is apples and oranges. But why can't we be blown away by both? Those of you who are parents may not need public recognition for when you parent creatively, but creative parenting does require a certain kind of brilliance.

* * *

So why can't the accountant be creative? If creativity is a *way* of doing things, then doesn't he just have to find *his* way? He just has to do his sums consciously, creatively, thoughtfully, and in the moment.

Once we change the rules, anyone who wants to play can play. It doesn't matter if you're a CEO or an assistant carpenter. It doesn't matter if you're setting a table or washing your car. If it's conscious and it's truly you, it becomes creative. It doesn't matter if you're making art or making sandwiches. It doesn't matter if you are making art that critics like or don't like. It doesn't matter if you're painting purple blobs dripping onto maroon Michelin tire retreads. Even if everyone hates it but it's giving you a sense of pleasure, then it's creative. If you're playing the guitar and only using minor chords because that is what moves you, then you're creating. Creative work cannot be judged. You cannot get an A in creativity. You also cannot get an F. No one can tell you you messed up. They can tell you they hate it. They can tell you they won't buy it. A critic could give it a bad review. But it's yours, and it comes from your open heart and your one-of-a-kind soul. If it turns you on, then it's creative.

I tell people on the first day of the workshop: "You can't be wrong in here. Your writing is *your* writing. This is writing from the heart; not writing from the Harvard degree. No one can tell you your work doesn't work. They can tell you it doesn't work for *them.* That's fine. Hopefully, you didn't write it for them.

Creativity is your soul expressing itself. I used to have trouble with the word *soul.* There really wasn't a definition for it, but after years of not knowing what to call my stuff that wasn't my body or my personality, I became comfortable with *soul.* My soul is my spirit and its nutrients are love and compassion and wisdom. And when it is filled, I am able to be a channel for those things. By *channel* I mean "conduit," as in "Nance, this is God speaking. I was wondering if I could borrow your self—that is, if you think you can relinquish your ego for an hour or two. I just want to pour some extreme love out there onto the desert and you're as good a pipeline as any."

And when my soul is empty I don't even hear the *Nance-this-is-God* part, and—worse—I start to think it's me doing the pouring. That's when I have to rely on the kindness of strangers and friends and trees and small animals to issue a there's-a-holier-than-thou-thing-going-around warning. I am told to take two slices of humble pie and not to bother calling anyone in the morning. That's when I know it's time to switch into creative gear. Creativity is the gasoline that fuels my spiritual engine. Creativity is soul food.

Creativity is a continuing process. And process and souls expressing themselves have nothing to do with selling or reviews or results or commercial success. They have everything to do with taking chances, being honest, letting us experiment with what feels right, letting ourselves make—as Anne Lamott brilliantly puts it in *Bird By Bird*—"shitty first drafts." This brainstorming of the gut will nourish your innards. Will it sell? Who knows?

If we all just give each other permission to be who we really are, the world would be just one huge art gallery. It's our one-of-a-kindness, our exquisite uniqueness, that odd twist of fate that shaped our individual bizarreness, that gives us everything we need to make great art. Giving that up, trying to please, masking our true beings is anticreative. But as my friend Gina said, people mess with your head if you're too original.

So what is the alternative? Make art by numbers? Color inside the lines? Die a little each day?

It's our authenticity, our originality, that is pure. If I'm afraid, then I can't let you see who I am, and then I'll do only the art you want me to. Creativity is maintaining the balance between the heart and the mind; the dedication to the moment and the ability to stand by and surrender and let the stuff flow through.

So plan to eat, drink, and be creative. And the minute you think two plus two equals four, take a hike.

So what about you? Maybe you're too busy. Maybe you're just scared. Maybe your creative fire got snuffed out. Maybe in second grade the art teacher looked at your drawing, appalled that you made your ocean orange. Or maybe when your Aunt Doris whispered to your mother, loud enough for you to hear, "Don't waste ballet lessons on her. She'll never be a dancer," you believed her. But that was then, and this is now. Don't give over your power so easily. Remember, you were the one who had the courage and the originality to not paint your ocean blue.

In my workshop I hear people say over and over how they used to write a lot and that when they read the stuff they wrote when they were younger, it actually was pretty good. They don't know why they stopped writing.

There are a million reasons why people stop doing what nourishes them. But there are another million why they can start up again.

So to all the artists in your painting studios, and to all the artists in your kitchen studios, and to every artist in between, start majoring in creativity. And sign up only for electives that promise to serve your soul.

EXERCISE:

Give yourself thirty minutes. Decide which ordinary thing you will turn into extraordinary. Turn something mundane into something holy. Then write about it. What was the experience like for you? How will you remember it? How will you change the channel from "what a drag" to "what a joy"?

Suggestions for soul-filling activities:

- Clean the hydrator in the refrigerator.
- Match all the socks in the sock drawer.
- Throw out all the stretched-out underwear that you never wear anymore.
- Organize your videotapes.
- Rip pages of a magazine and make a collage that says *I am creativity.*
- Add a plant to your work area.
- Make an exotic mushroom sandwich on toasted country French bread. Serve it to yourself on your prettiest plate with a yellow and orange nasturtium.
- Put a love note under the pillow of someone you love.

Remember, It's a Leap—Not a Schlep

Writing for a Change

My friend Maryanne, a psychologist, says transitions are the hardest times for people. She says transitions are difficult because they make you face the unknown. When catastrophe strikes, people choose to stay stuck in the misery they know because *knowing* is easier than not knowing.

Culturally, we Westerners have a much harder time with change because we are raised to think everything should stay hunky-dory, and when it doesn't, we are convinced we are just the one unlucky slob that the fickle finger of dumpage has found. I credit all those children's stories that end with "and they all lived happily ever after." I bought it; you probably did too. Look at the energy we spend trying to live "happily ever after" as opposed to "not too bad right now."

I remember the first time I opened M. Scott Peck's *The Road Less*

Traveled. The first line on the first page in the first chapter is "Life is difficult." I promptly slammed the book shut and went to get a little bite. I didn't want to read about how life is difficult. I wanted the grown-up version of "happily ever after." I continued my search for the perpetual *My Little Margie,* the comforting sparkle of Doris Day, and the dimpled assurance of Debbie Reynolds all rolled into one romantic comedy that would be my life.

The stark reality is, nothing is permanent. Everything changes. I will never forget watching a Tibetan monk making his mandala sandpainting at Trinity College in Hartford, Connecticut. *Mandala* is Sanskrit for circle. It's the symbolic diagram of the universe in Chinese, Japanese, and Tibetan art. This monk worked every day for five months. He was a generous spirit with twinkling eyes and an infectious giggle. He would let anyone who wanted to—especially the children—add some of the beautiful colored sand to the piece. He would show us how to shake the *raghok* (the tool) and then we'd step behind the ropes again and know that we had contributed to this holy, one-of-a-kind work of art. When he finished, there was a big celebration. And then the most remarkable thing happened. We all followed him to the edge of the Farmington River and watched in mixed horror and awe as he threw the completed painting into the raging waters. He was teaching us that we can't hold on to anything, that whatever we are doing—even the breath we are taking—is already over. By destroying the mandala, we got to witness this perfect expression of impermanence.

* * *

Transition is the shedding of the snakeskin. You don't hear the snake saying, "I can't let go of the whole thing. I just need to keep a little clump—just in case." Nature has the thing designed to perfection. Transitions are less painful if we remember that it's a leap, not a schlep.

Transitions are those in-between places where you've got one foot in the old life, and one foot poised—but not quite set down—in the new life. Transition is the gray between "was married" and "now divorced." Graduating college kids experience transition when they leave home and school for the first time and enter the "real world." Transition is also going from being Mom to empty nest. Transition is going from when you *thought* fifty was old, to when you knew being sixty included sagging breasts, liver spots, double chins. Transition is the "golden years" tarnishing—where two of your closest friends just died, another one of them can't remember your name, and memorizing the obituary page has replaced scanning the front page.

Transition is a death of sorts. And from our culture, we have learned, above all, to fear death. Our funerals are tragic events filled with whispers and sobs. We don't talk about death. We have no ritual around death. Most of us have no rite of passage to teach us about death. Think about it. We put our old people away so we don't have to see what the "beginning" of death looks like.

I have two young women friends, sisters, in their twenties. When they were five and seven, their mother died suddenly. Their uncle (their mother's brother) came to their elementary school and brought them home without saying a word. He sat them down and, with his back to them, said, "Your mother is with the angels and now you are going to live with us." All their things were moved, and they were never allowed to talk about their mother again. It was as if she had never existed.

We must honor the fact that there is a time to live and a time to die. Transitions are teachers, and yet look how much energy we spend struggling to avoid this difficult dance.

Joseph Campbell wrote

If the seed does not die
there is no plant

Bread results
from the death of wheat

Life lives on lives

Writing during a transition is the bridge that helps you get from the known to the unknown. It is the high-intensity filament that lights your way across the abyss and over to the other side. It is your best friend, your sounding board, sitting with you until the dawn breaks.

Words forge the path that will take you to the place your mind and your hurting heart are afraid to go. Without thinking, analyzing, philosophizing, every step of the terrified way, without all those trained-to-behave-the-way-they-always-have neurons pumping, without judgment, comes clarification. And there you have it—staring at you from the page, telling you where you've been and escorting you gently to where you're going. Writing is your guide to knowing your self. And guess what? The wisdom is your own. It comes from the deepest interior of your psyche, where bravery dwells. It comes from your truth.

May Sarton, the author of *Journal of a Solitude*, says, "Go deep enough and there is a bedrock of truth, however hard." And I say it's been sitting there waiting for you to run out of places to hide in as you continue your frantic search for easy solutions. It's been waiting for you to turn off the television, to close the magazine, to stop scrubbing the rust stain in the sink. It's been waiting for you to sit still and be ready. It's been waiting for you to make the scariest leap of all—the leap into the unknown. In Joseph Campbell's *Reflections*, he tells of a young Native American who, at the time of his initiation, is advised

As you go the way of life,
you will see a great chasm.

Jump

It is not as wide as you think.

Writing narrows the chasm. Writing gets you ready for your initiation. Writing gets you ready for the "hero's journey."

You've heard people who have had spiritual epiphanies after the worst tragedies of their lives. They were forced to go inside because they couldn't find any answers on the outside. Caroline Myss, author of *Anatomy of the Spirit*, says, "No one takes up the bed and walks unless it's gotten uncomfortable." She means unless someone we don't like has moved into the bed with us, we won't change.

We don't go looking for transition. Transition crashes in on our cozy nests and we are thrown out onto the street to crawl in the gutter, to double over in pain, to carry the full weight of confusion everywhere we go. Transition is an opportunity to take the call. But not everyone does.

In my workshop, women in their fifties sometimes write about the adventures they didn't take because they were too frightened. After they remember the experiences they passed up, the relationships they turned down, the trips they canceled, they write them down on paper. It seems that people who are fifty and older who take the workshop go through a whole grieving process over their lives unlived, or lived for others. First they tell themselves all the reasons why they couldn't have possibly gone, next they get angry at their husbands or wives who have been such creeps to have not supported them, their mothers who had strokes just as they were about to leave on their vision quest to the top of Kilimanjaro.

Then they allow themselves to feel the loss. Once they have proof on paper of what they missed, they are ready for the call next time. Then they have what Margaret Mead calls *PMZ* (post-menopausal zest). That's when the writing turns a corner. Using the power and the wisdom and the sudden willingness to celebrate this last transition, they write like they've never written before.

For my mother's seventy-fifth birthday, I promised her I would invite her bridge club out to my Vineyard cabin for the weekend. There were two Beas, one Sarah, and my Henny. We're talking women in their late seventies. One couldn't eat greasy (she gets heartburn); one couldn't eat dairy (she gets stomach cramps); one couldn't eat peppers (she burps); one couldn't sit without pillows (she needs to prop her hip).

They were sad about what they no longer could do, but they were adorable about all they still could and would do. We talked about subjects I thought these women would never discuss. We talked about affairs not had, chances not taken, dreams not fulfilled. They were courageous and intelligent and direct and funny.

At one point we were playing the board game Scruples, where the choices are "yes," "no," or "depends." This was the question Bea Number One got: "You are at a dinner party and hear a distinct crack as a corpulent guest settles into an antique chair. The hostess is in the kitchen. Will you tell her what happened?" Bea Number One immediately says,"Depends," and we all challenge her, asking, "Depends on what?" Without a trace of hesitation, Bea says, "Depends on who my friend is—the hostess or the fat behind." We roared!

The honesty and love that I saw and felt reinforced what I already know is the most vital ingredient in our lives: telling our truths. These women have been transitioning for years. They taught me that it was a leap—not a schlep.

In my workshop I see men and women in their thirties and forties, and—most shockingly—in their twenties, writing their hearts out (or, as I prefer to call it, writing their hearts "in"), telling their stories, making the connections between their childhood wounds and their adult behavior. I watch their determination to feel and to deal, and then to heal, so there won't be a busy signal the next time they get a call.

Writing connects the cable so you can hear that call. When people in my workshops write "the revelatory piece," I hear them say over and over again, "I don't know where *that* came from." Or, "I can't believe I remembered that," or "I didn't even know I knew that." They say this about memories, about insights, and about their own pure inner wisdom that comes bubbling up to meet their sorrow.

Ralph Waldo Emerson said, "What lies behind us and what lies before us are tiny matters compared to what lies within us." Writing invites you to search deeper to access what lies within you. Writing answers your questions—the ones you are afraid to ask and the ones you have been asking all your life. You've always known the answers; writing helps you *know* you know them.

In the middle of an actual transition, you might not even be able to write a complete sentence. Your mind is fully focused on survival, your body is on automatic, and your heart is on shutdown for the season. That's when it's important to get a thought, a phrase, a paragraph down on paper. Some gem of prophetic lucidity might pop out totally uncensored, *plunk* in the center of the turmoil-swirl. Suppose you just got laid off from your fifteen-year corporate climb. You were making good money, you had your routine, your life, your plan in place. In three minutes, all of that was obliterated, and all that remains is a crumbling immobilized package of insecurity with a closet full of silk blouses. "Who am I?" you may write. "What am I going to do? Who's going to hire me? I hated the stupid job anyway. I hated rush-hour traffic. I hated the smell of the carpet. I hated microwaving my lunch. I hated those demeaning evaluations. I should just jump off a building. I should just open a kitchen shop. I'll show those calculating creeps."

Three years later, when you are sitting in your sweet little kitchen shop one brisk mile walk away from your apartment admiring its beautiful bare oak floors, eating your nine-grain bread, goat cheese, and alfalfa sprout sandwich (unnuked), being your own boss, you will flip back through the pages of your nightmare and read the lifeline you unconsciously threw to yourself. The point is, you don't have to write perfect prose during the transition. Let the part of you that can still breathe do the writing. Transition writing is not so much art as it is survival.

Writing the truth of our "transition journeys" is the gift we give to ourselves and to each other, the gift that says, "You are not alone." There is no separateness. Only the details are different. I see it over and over again in my groups when the first person finds the courage to tell her story. It only takes about two seconds for everyone else to think, "If she can read *hers* then I can write *mine*. . . ."

EXERCISE:

Write about a transition you have completed. Include how you felt before, during, and after.

Write a paragraph describing a transition you are in now.

Take this current transition and write a ritual ceremony. You are the person going through the rite of passage. Write the monologue the chief elder gives to you at this crucial time.

It's Open Season for Metaphor Hunting

If you had asked me, when I was a child, to give a generic description of a teacher, I would have said someone who wears nice clothes, stands in front of the room next to the chalkboard, and knows everything. As I grew older my definition expanded, and then much later, I realized my own children held graduate degrees in my most relevant course of study—life. My perceptions went splat on the sidewalk right there on the corner of Main Street and Paradigm Avenue. I realized my lessons could come from everywhere and anywhere. A teacher could wear anything—sit, stand, or fly—and there didn't have to be a blackboard.

However, *understanding* a concept and *living* a concept are two very different matters. So even though I thought I was open and receptive, I'm sure I yawned and ignored and missed truckloads of gold because the teacher didn't look the part. It's funny how wisdom works in reverse.

As a child I had inherent wisdom, and even though my information was limited, my intuition wasn't, so I judged nothing and accepted everything. Then, as an adult, when my cynicism and fear kicked in, I rejected anything that seemed "far out." The more I knew intellectually, the less I knew innately. By the time I was thirty, my rules for knowing were rigid. My reality margins were closing in on themselves. Pretty soon I would have one thin column of acceptable, widely held perceptions. How odd in an era where the information highway was adding a new passing lane every hour!

My role in my life (and anyone else's life I could get my hands on) had always been the controller. I was about to do my number again in the middle of a phone conversation one Sunday morning, when instead I surrendered the receiver to my husband.

I walked out into the garden, lecturing myself. *There I go again,* I thought. I was just about to argue for a plan that I shouldn't even have been involved in. I thought, *This controlling hasn't helped anyone. So why do I do it?* My answer came quickly: *Because it makes me feel powerful.* And then it hit me—control isn't power; it's fear. Real power is letting go.

At that moment, my eyes fell on the dense patch of yellow coreopsis blooming in full sunlight at the border of my garden. There were hundreds of them—bright yellow double daisies reaching for the sun. But when I looked closer, many of them were bent and twisted by coiling tendrils of heavenly blue morning glories. Morning glories climb anything. They will circle and wrap around the tallest thing they can find. They'll look for rope, poles, and stray branches. If a gladiolus is dumb enough to grow too close, they'll even use her. They'll reach for anything they can twist themselves around to get their nourishment. The coreopsis were being choked by the morning glories. So here were two beautiful flowers, but because one needed to entwine itself around the other to get where it was going, it was killing its support system. And *I* was the gardener. I could have staked the tall, spindly, golden babies so they wouldn't have been so weak and I could have built a trellis so the heavenly blues would have had a better place to grow. I stood there as if the genie had just popped out of the proverbial bottle and with a flourish of his hands had said, "Nance! You got it! The control thing!" So I was getting a visual demonstration, a metaphor growing right there in my garden, of what I was doing to my marriage—and all my other relationships as well. Health had just hit me square between the eyes.

The whole thing was so exciting, I ran in to tell my husband the miracle of the metaphor. He had long since hung up and was back to reading his *Scientific American.* I said, "Babe, I just had a huge revelation about us. You know how I've always needed to control everything?" He looked up at me a bit baffled, said *he* hadn't thought there had been an imbalance of power, and went on reading about the existence of seismic anistrophy. I decided it would be controlling to get him to stop reading his article so he could get excited about my psychological discovery. So I let it go.

Now we make a very balanced couple if you think of yin as being blown away by flower metaphors and yang as wondering what force is keeping those iron hexagons in such close alignment.

* * *

Last November, a friend who is in her fifties and I were walking on the side of the road talking about getting older. She said she had been getting depressed lately because she hated looking in the mirror and seeing this "old lady." We were randomly picking flowers and weeds while we were walking. I said I was happier now than I was when I was younger. She said, "Me, too, except I hate it that my skin is drying up and my eyes are sagging and my flesh is hanging." We agreed that the phrase "Youth is wasted on the young" is one of the most meaningful lines ever uttered. Then she said, "And you don't even know what it means till you've lost it. Oh, my god, I sound like my mother." There was a silence. It was a moment of understanding that the wand was being passed, both of us knowing that if we took it we were leaving a certain young girl behind. This young girl was stupid, had made stupid mistakes, was caught up in her own little life, but she was all innocence, and we never realized how beautiful her skin was until now. On the other hand, this mother we were about to become had learned a few things, was ready to let go of a bunch of things, saw a much larger *what's-it-all-about-Alfie* picture, but the looking glass for reflection was the place we'd look for answers.

We talked about our youth-obsessed culture and our collective cultural terror about getting old. We each kept only one flower we had picked to bring home. When we got back to our car, we examined what each of us had chosen. She had a new bud. Its tender leaves hadn't begun to unfurl. It held promise. It was perfect, as if someone had designed the most exquisite way to be a flower. We were struck by the innocence of it, the sheer power of a thing not yet realized, its whole unfolding ahead of it. Because we knew what was coming, and the flower did not.

Then we looked at the one I was holding. It was brown; it was dead. It had had its moment in the sun. But in its death there was a combination of fragility and power we recognized as beautiful, but hadn't seen yet in our own selves. The pale, pale, see-through petals had hung on like a remnant of old lace clinging for dear life to an old bent curtain rod in an abandoned window somewhere. It was shaky and vulnerable, but the thing hadn't fallen from the tree; it had hung in there through all the summer and fall storms. Together we sighed, and we both knew we were sighing for our buds that had flowered. But we also knew that we were trading glowing skin for shining wisdom.

So there you have it: metaphors galore. These would-be lessons, these eye openers, not only give meaning and deepen our lives, but they are invitations to delve into life's mysteries, which cannot be fathomed with theorems and formulas. And you become the recipient.

Writers need to dig. Writers need to dive below the calm surface. We have to break through to as many realities as we can. We have to push past conventional wisdom and see how staying neatly within the borders limits our work, and keeps it safe and generic.

Look at the world as a constant kaleidoscope with new configurations happening every time the slightest bit of data is altered. The rational mind is a prison for poetry. Writing is not an intellectual pursuit. Your voice is the only voice like it; your take on the world is the only take like it. The brain can have its say, but as a writer, don't give it that much power. When you create, you must go around and beyond and behind and under and through. All the censors in the world are just sitting in wait so they can nab you and give you a ticket for driving on the wrong side of the brain.

That's where your one-of-a-kind voice is waiting to surface. And you are the only one who can throw it a line.

EXERCISE:

Write one metaphor. Then see if it is your morning-glory story.

Beware of the Hexpert

I tell my students to call themselves writers if they are writing. After all, if you write, then you're a writer. If you sing, then you're a singer. If you paint, then you're a painter.

I don't know who it was who made the rule that you had to be published to be called a writer and or have a gig at Carnegie Hall to be called a singer or get the Museum of Modern Art to come to your studio and beg you to let them show one of your pieces to be called a painter.

It took me several lifetimes and many bylines until I could deal with the dreaded "And what do you do?" so that I could say, "I'm a writer." I know how strange it felt in my mouth, how disconnected I was to such a phrase. So, in case you haven't already given yourself permission, take permission gently from one who has been there. You're writing? You're a writer.

But, remember there is always the danger when naming or labeling of limiting rather than expanding your self. With labels come expectations, and with expectations comes pressure. My grandmother used to pronounce expert with an *H.* Maybe it wasn't a language deficiency; maybe she was making a commentary.

So forget everything I said about calling yourself a writer. Call yourself a perpetual butterfly always in transformation, call yourself a Tiffany lamp, call yourself a cat in its eighth life. Better yet, don't call yourself. Wait, and you will hear the call.

The label thing is dangerous because when you think you're a *whatever*-your-label-is, then you have to be a *whatever* expert. And when you're an expert, there's no room for error. There's no chance for discovery. There's no "anything-is-possible" because the expert has explored all the possibilities and the expert knows exactly how it should be done. Gone is the magic. Gone is the spontaneity. Gone is the mistake that often becomes the best art. Experts don't make mistakes. Just ask an expert seamstress how to sew, and she will tell you there's only one way and she knows it. Just ask a dishwasher expert how to load, and he will give you a set of directions that don't include any variations on his theme.

Wayne Dyer, who wrote *You Have To Believe It To See It,* tells the story of the "expert" Buddhist from the West who announces to everyone he meets how much he knows about Buddhism. He talks incessantly about karma and meditation and mindfulness and yoga and the nature of selflessness. One day he gets the chance to travel to India to meet his guru. He's thrilled to be in the presence of such a great man. He sits and begins talking. He tells the guru everything he knows about Buddhism and the teacher listens and listens. And the man keeps talking, showing the teacher all he knows. Finally the teacher interrupts and asks him if he would like some tea and the man says, "Oh, yes, that would be very nice." And the man continues talking. The teacher brings the tea tray and begins pouring the tea into the man's cup. The man continues talking. When the cup is filled, the teacher keeps pouring. The tea is running onto the table and pretty soon it is spilling onto the floor and then onto the man's pants leg and the man keeps talking but he is starting to freak out a bit and finally, at long last, he stops and he says, "Why are you pouring more tea? My cup is already filled." The teacher stops pouring and says, "You are like the cup. You are filled so there is no room for any more."

I have suffered from the filled-to-the-brim syndrome. I'm convinced it should be included in psychology books under *extremely terrified.*

When my need to be an authority becomes greater than my willingness to keep growing, it's a big clue for me to get quiet. Go deep. Get scared.

Living creatively for me means being willing to screw up, to play the fool, now and again. I don't mean being a stupid fool—the butt of the practical joke, the slapstick clown—but instead the one who makes the error, the one who can be wrong, the one who understands he will mess up, the one who doesn't know everything, the one who can be lost. Because I know that my biggest mistakes become my best teachers, and my biggest mistake might be my best piece of work. Of course, it's not really a mistake. It's just the moment I get out of my own way. It's the moment my ego takes a coffee break.

Children are the perfect nonexperts. They play the fool willingly. They don't think, *Oh, I'm so embarrassed. I don't think I look very smooth getting onto my Hot Wheels. And besides, I'm not very good at it.* They have innate curiosity, and innate understanding that failures are just as important as successes. They couldn't name a failure if it jumped up and bit them. They don't label things. They have no censors. They don't go around depressed because they haven't gotten as far along as they had anticipated in their version of "Twinkle, Twinkle" on their half-sized violins. They want to try everything because they're the consummate beginners. They have a natural competitive spirit, competing with their own record. They know how good it feels when they get better at something. But they couldn't have a conversation about it. "Oh, yeah. I got rid of my training wheels. I'm feeling really good about myself for having stuck it out." They don't get arrogant, they get confident.

Every morning I would bake a cake for my classes. I was never a baker; I hate measuring and timing things. But just when my writers' tummies are starting to fill with doubt, I like to have something warm and sweet for them to eat. I would be right in the middle of making a recipe and suddenly realize that I didn't have milk, so I would have to substitute yogurt and it would come out better. Or when I ran out of vanilla I would use almond extract, and it turned out like a gourmet dessert of the month. Now I have somewhat of a routine, but still there's always something different. Some are winners, and some provide us with the heartiest laugh of the day. One time the cake just wouldn't coagulate (I know this is not a baking term) and finally, after it had been in the oven on three hundred degrees for two hours, I took it out and served it with spoons. We called it "almond pudding," and everyone wanted the same thing the next day. Of course I couldn't reproduce it. After all, it was a piece of art, and you can't reproduce art. As soon as you do, it's not art; it's product. And the last thing I want to do for writers working on process is manufacture product for their morning treat.

So how come there are so many experts? I learned at a young and tender age that admitting I didn't know was one of life's bigger sins. So right off the beginner's bat, I was in expert training. I knew I needed lots of "how-tos" so I wouldn't be caught being a beginner again. Then I could always look accomplished. What I didn't learn was the trade-off: my safety for my soul. Finding the balance between knowing something, being thoroughly accomplished in something, and being open to new information helps not only my heart but my writing from the heart.

If you are hanging on to the expert in yourself, at least let him (or her) go out for some Ovaltine when you sit down to write. Let your mind be the empty teacup, let your heart be full of love, and let your precious work come through.

EXERCISE:

Write about a time you were the filled teacup. What was the area of expertise?

Now write a piece about a time when you were a beginner.

MY FIRST
car
experience with death
boyfriend
joint
girlfriend
apartment
kiss
root canal

cheeseburger
bee sting
oyster
visit to the emergency room
orgasm
crush
success

The Evil Editor with the Bad Marriage

The day after I got a form letter of rejection from the *New York Times Magazine* column *Lives,* I sat at my desk and flipped through the pages of the March *Victoria's Secret* catalog. I'll show them, I thought. I'll order twenty of those second-skin satin bras, for my sexy, sultry, sensuous body, which is now in a permanent state of mourning.

I loved that story. It was a good story; it was funny. It was me. *Who are these idiots, anyway?* I think. And as fast as it takes me to switch from a hunter green demi-bra to a deep teal padded pushup, I go from *What do they know anyway*? to *I don't deserve to buy anything because* a) *I have no right to purchase when I have no talent, and I can't even earn a meager living as a writer, and besides—I have nowhere to go, anyway*; and b) *there is no b.*

Rejection sucks. It's as simple as that.

I'd like to tell you rejection makes you stronger, that it builds character, that it makes great interview material for when your best-seller comes out and you can tell Barbara Walters, "I got fourteen rejections before Viking took a chance on me."

But the fact is, there's nothing okay about it. And the bigger fact is, if rejection stops you in your tracks, you should keep your day job. Security at the top of your life priority list secures nothing but your litany of limitations, which will not only always be there, but as long as you give them room and board, they will begin to furnish the space with their Oriental threadbare rugs and their faded chipped Hummell dolls. Uncle Harry will always be in your head telling you, "You're too smart for your own good." (Has anyone figured out what that actually means?) And when Uncle Harry quiets down, Miss Baroley from eighth grade will segue into her lecture, beginning with the words, "You'll never amount to anything." When you have put arsenic in her Diet Coke, David Weinstock will take over asking, "Who do you think you are?" This for-your-head-only theatrical presentation will continue until you decide you're in charge.

The thing I had to learn was that it is only one person who is doing the rejecting. One single entity, who reads your work and makes a decison, holds your life in his or her hands. You are subject to what he ate for breakfast, what kind of a fight she had with her kid, and scariest of all possiblities—that she wishes she had written it herself.

So if you want, you can be the victim of the evil editor with the bad marriage. Or you can think, *Maybe it's the work, but it only needs a bit more attention.* Or you can think, *It's the work and it's really garbage and if anyone deserved a big fat rejection, it is me.* Here is one time where the truth is not important. What is important is to figure out what will get you back to writing the quickest.

I was on a softball team a few years ago. It was the first team I had ever been on. They needed four women to qualify in the league, so I was actually a valued player. Not because I was good, but because, as they put it when they recruited me, "We need four girls, and you're a girl." The coach would yell insults during the games, and at practice he would single each one of us out and hurl hurtful vicious comments. I was just recovering from the "Aronie, what're ya on, horse tranquilizers?" line, when I asked the two guys standing with me, "Does this kind of abuse motivate you?" Both of them nodded enthusiastically. "What is it about being insulted that makes you want to work harder?" I asked. They answered almost simultaneously. It was the *I'll-show-him* syndrome. Maybe it's a guy thing or a sports thing, but I told them it was the opposite for me. If I am encouraged, I said, I want to please the encourager. If I am put down, I'm likely to stay down. So for me, when the rejection comes, it's probably best if I think the editor has a really bad life, hates his wife, and didn't even read my piece. Otherwise I'll spend the rest of my writing life in a hole looking up and waiting for the second shoe to drop. It's so easy to avoid the working anyway, but after a rejection, it's almost impossible to resist the resistance.

After all, why write? Why do anything no one appreciates? If there's no one in the forest, can you hear a tree fall? If there's no one loving your precious pearls, can you hear a tree fall or write a poem about it?

BEN AND JERRY'S CHERRY GARCIA

You may not be in charge of whether the piece gets published, but you are in charge of what you do with the rejection. I suggest eating Ben and Jerry's Cherry Garcia ice cream. As someone in my workshop pointed out: Who are they kidding, four servings per container? The carton is the only way to go. Or, if you're in touch with your higher self—golly—go run five miles through verdant green forests and thank your inner wisdom for protecting you from premature success. You could fall victim to what I refer to with my younger students as the "Kurt Cobain" syndrome: too big too fast and not enough spiritual preparation. That's too glib for such a tragedy, but looking at a rejection from a Zen standpoint, you can say, "I'm honoring my journey, and this rejection is part of it," and then you can gluttonize the entire container of Cherry Garcia.

If you are willing to take the risk of being authentic, which means doing your own work and transcending the fear (for the minute) of not being perfect, and you are starting to send stuff out, the chances are that rejection will be a big part of your writing life. It's an occupational hazard. In some jobs, you can lose a leg. In this job, you can lose faith, confidence, self-esteem, ground, enthusiasm, and the only thing you've ever really wanted to do.

MOPPING AND GLOWING

In our first session of each of my workshops, I hear over and over again, "I used to want to be a writer," or "I used to do a lot of writing." If our educational system valued the arts or if we all had a mentor, we would learn that doing art is hard, that we will come upon a million blocks and impasses in the middle of the road, that that's part of the deal and it's okay to take a break, that it's okay to stop for a bit, but to call it what it is: stopping. People who stop along the way for whatever reason think they have quit, as if there's some kind of professional writing rule that they have no right to reenter the game. Instead, consider it a hiatus. You went on holiday. You raised a child. You were making a living. You were mopping and glowing. It doesn't matter. You can do all those things and come back and do your art. You don't have to quit. You don't have to apologize; you don't have to think you're indulging yourself. You just have to find out if you want to write again, and then you have to do it.

DARK TUESDAY

Transition is a great word to use if people want to know what's happening to you. *I'm in transition.* I wish I had known that word when, in 1988, National Public Radio dumped me out of the blue. I had been doing commentaries for them on a regular freelance basis. I would write the piece, call them, read it to the producer. He would say, "You're unbelievable,"- and I would grow ten feet tall. Then I would tape the piece and it would be on the air and everyone in my town would tell me I was great and I would grow twenty feet tall. I didn't get arrogant; I just got confident. That's fair. Everyone deserves a hit of confidence. But I called one Tuesday—Dark Tuesday—and they said I had been dropped from the roster. No explanation, no reason, no apology. I remember phoning my husband at work and telling him he had to come home; I was dying. I walked around the bedroom doubled over, gasping.

I had just begun to garden. I had grown a small patch of cosmos on the side of my house, but I was always reticent to pick them because they looked so beautiful outside. I couldn't bear to pick the few that were waving in the gentle breeze in my very first tiny garden. So I bought flowers from a stand and put them in vases dotted around my house. Then my friend Marcy came over and I confessed to her that the flowers in the house were store-bought and we had ourselves a good beginner-gardener laugh. She explained to me that if you want flowers to flourish, you have to pinch them back. You have to pick them, and more and bigger ones will grow. She said flowers beget flowers.

So now NPR had pinched me back, cut me down, forced my growth. This was good, I said to myself as I held my aching stomach. This is good for the garden, I thought as I held back the terrified tears. I would grow from this. I would become a bigger blossom. Then I wailed to the empty hallways in my house, "I am not a flower. I am not a garden. I am a fragile human being who has just been knifed in the gut and I am going to bleed to death!"

My husband came home, and since he was just beginning to learn how to hold me and not think he had to solve everything, he tried his best. Little by little, I survived. I don't know if a bigger bloom came or not. I know I found some compost elsewhere, and I'm still a member in good standing of the garden club.

Then lo and behold, after two years, I submitted a piece to NPR and they aired it immediately. As abruptly as I was eliminated, I was reinstated. So as my gramma always said, "Go know."

The hard part about rejection is that we all want its opposite—acceptance. We've already been rejected, standing on the outside looking in, banging on the window of their hearts. And since we think our writing is an extension of who we are, it feels as if it is *you*, instead of your work, who is being rejected.

MISS CONVIVIALITY, AND QUEEN OF EVERYTHING

Now, on a day when you're feeling pretty okay—not too high, not too low—can you look at what made you a writer in the first place? Chances are it wasn't because you got Most Popular and Best Dressed and were crowned Queen of Everything. Chances are you've been on the outside before, and it's what taught you your compassion, gave you your pain, your ability to know and understand the human condition. So it isn't an accident that now you are able to write it (draw it, paint it, sculpt it). It's this very vulnerability, this very pain of being left out, different, alone, rejected that makes your writing work. So it isn't that you want to trade and become Miss Conviviality all of a sudden; it's just—How about a little recognition to get me through the decade?

MR. AND MRS. TOXIC

So we've established that rejection stings and we don't want it anywhere near us, but when it happens (because it will), what are we going to do? We are going to get as much nourishment as we can from other sources that will help remind us that we are on individual journeys that may not include getting published in the *New York Times*.

Please hang in there. Call your best friend. Cry, moan, bitch, and call your next best friend. Do not call Mr. and Mrs. Toxic. They will not make you feel better, and if you have deluded yourself into thinking this time will be different, I'm here to tell ya, it won't. *They won't tell me if I just applied myself a little more, if I just had some discipline, if I just stopped hanging around those loser friends of mine, if I just lost weight, if I just* . . . Because if you keep calling Mr. and Mrs. Toxic, you might as well get *two* containers of Ben and Jerry's.

Better you should go for a walk in nature. Talk to a tree. Pick up your pen, turn on your computer, plug in your laptop, and start all over again.

EXERCISES:

Open a book at random and pick a line you like, any line. Use it as your first line in a piece about anything. This doesn't have to have a beginning or an end. Just write for about an hour and see where it goes.

Write a piece that starts with the words *I reject rejection because* . . . Spend no more than thirty minutes on this.

Then write for thirty more: *I embrace rejection because* . . .

Write a poem that begins:

> *Roses are red*
> *Violets are bluish. . . .*

Here's my ending:

> *They rejected my piece*
> *Because I am Jewish?*

Now, you make up your own.

Mentors and Mensches

I didn't know a person could become a writer. I had never seen one.

When I was in tenth grade, I had a drama teacher who loved her job. She would come sweeping into class carrying props and books and scripts and notes and those mint chocolate girl scout cookies that you could only get in the month of March. She was tiny, but her energy was enormous.

Half the kids in the class were genuinely interested in theater and the other half were there because they had heard it was an easy credit.

So the hoods and the bohemians, the beatniks and the gangsters, the "smart" kids and the "dumb" kids, were all thrown together. Any other teacher would have found this combination disastrous. But immediately she had us mesmerized, and we knew we had finally found the exception to our thus far boring educational experience.

Miss Kreiger would run up and down the aisles holding a playbook at arm's length, her glasses perched on the end of her turned up little nose as she performed scenes from *A Streetcar Named Desire, A Raisin in the Sun,* and *A View from the Bridge.* Her arms flailing, her mouth puckering, her eyebrows dancing, she would stop and abruptly hand the book to one of us to pick up where she'd left off. It wasn't that she wanted to catch you off guard; in fact, she'd always somehow let you know that you might be the next one called. When she gave the book to the scariest kid in our whole town—the one who had stayed back a minimum of fourteen times, who we were convinced was at least thirty-three years old, she would say things like, "Oooh, listen to that perfect accent—say that again, Tony! Was your mother from Italy? Oh I see, just your grandmother," or, "Oh, my God! That's beautiful. You're soooo lucky you have an authentic Italian grandmother."

You knew in the fifties, in our land of assimilation, that Tony had never been told that having an "authentic Italian grandmother" was a *good* thing. I was actually seeing the validation of another human being—and in school, of all places. Before that, the teaching tools for motivation I had most often seen were intimidation, humiliation, and shame.

So Miss Kreiger directed *You Can't Take It with You,* a play about a lovable wacky family, and she cast the other toughest guy in school as the lead. Rehearsals were what I'd imagined college would be like. We'd stay late at school, feeding each other our lines and slices of cold pizza that Miss Kreiger had paid for with her own money and had let us pick up in her own car.

She always ate with us, and one night she told us about a little basement theater in New York that no one knew about and another one that was in a condemned building on Avenue D. Just the idea of a going to a play in a *condemned building* was romantic. She said tickets to Eugene O'Neill's *Long Day's Journey into Night* were twenty-five cents! And then all of a sudden her eyes would take on this glazed look as she would break into a mini-performance:

> It was like walking on the bottom of the sea. As if I had drowned long ago. . . . As if I was a ghost belonging to the fog, and the fog was the ghost of the sea. It felt damned peaceful to be nothing more than a ghost within a ghost.

Then she would linger and pause and snap out of it and say, "That's the speech that Edmund makes right after the wine and roses part." And then she would sigh, and there would be silence. Who ever heard a teacher sigh? Who ever sat with a teacher in silence?

She told us some of the best acting was happening in basements and lofts. She told us how, even though the family in our play was nuts and even though they didn't do things conventionally, they loved each other and that that was the most important thing. And you knew she wasn't just talking about the play.

Miss Kreiger was never condescending. It was her respect for us—for all of us—that made us realize that the black turtleneck jerseys we wore to be like real Greenwich Village actors were exactly like the black turtleneck jerseys the hoods were wearing to be just like Marlon Brando. She showed us that when people are treated with respect, they act respectfully. She gave us the chance to see ourselves in each other.

But the most important contribution Miss Kreiger made was her passion. We had never seen passion. We were fourteen, and we lived in a passionless world. I was seeing an adult who was not only marching to the tune of her own drummer, but wildly dancing to it.

It turned out that the play was a spectacular success. It dumped the school on its clique-ridden head. Even the principal stood up and congratulated the black-leather-jacket crowd. At our curtain call, there was a thunderous standing ovation that felt as if it would last till graduation.

Miss Kreiger was the first "eccentric" I had ever known. She wore unteacherish clothes, she drove an un-grown-up's car, she wore big dangly earrings, and she ate food in front of us. In 1957, you never saw teachers eat. You could see how nervous certain people got in her presence and how inspired others would get. You also knew she wasn't doing anything to make a statement or start a rebellion; she was just being herself.

I was so drawn to it. I knew I was seeing something important. But my whole programming dictated that eccentricity was a negative, a show-offy cry for attention. It was acceptable in the entertainment world—like a Liberace affectation kind of a thing. *He* wasn't a threat to the members of the town council. But a local eccentric had to be made safe, and the only way to do that was to label her "the nut," to put up with the foolishness and to write it off as crazy but harmless.

From my young eyeballs, people all looked the same. From my young gut, I felt different. Here was a woman saying that different was not only okay—it was special.

I recently learned that *eccentric* means "away from the center." Everyone would be eccentric if we weren't so afraid of the consequences. The punishment in our civilized society for not joining the center is to be ostracized. And what is this center that is so revered? It is the force that pulls us back from our own creativity, our own voices, our own uniqueness.

If there weren't such a value on sameness—if we finally figured out how alike we really are underneath the masks of our own making—I think we would be more than willing to give each other the leeway to explore who's *in* there so we could develop and celebrate our own authentic selves. Writing is a chance to be real. How can you turn this invitation down? The expense of not accepting such an invitation is too great. Saying, "No, I'd rather be who you need me to be," causes illness of the heart, the soul, and the body.

Imagine if we valued imagination. Then everyone would be eccentric. Everyone would be able to go "out there," which of course is really "in there." Everyone would be the piece of art they were meant to be.

I didn't know it then, but Miss Kreiger was a mentor for me.

Mentors change lives. They sprinkle fairy mist on parched souls. I would have died without the oasis she provided.

Mentors help you keep your dream alive. In primitive times, the old people were the ones who were the guardians of the mysteries and the laws. But now our old people are in nursing homes, with no such responsiblity. They have all the time in the world to sit alone and forget.

Everyone should have a mentor, and a mentor can be anybody. He doesn't need a degree in mentoring; he or she just needs to be a mensch.

Mensch is Yiddish for a person who is good—who has a good soul, who has a good heart. A mentor-mensch would be a good person who still has his "thrill gene" intact. My friend Dana, who teaches music in the inner city, calls it a "transference of fire." That's what Miss Kreiger did for me; she transferred her fire.

Teachers and parents are so burned out today that kids are being shortchanged. They aren't living in the presence of live passion. MTV is no substitute. The spectacle of multimillion-dollar movies is no substitute. Radio talk show hosts railing against each other is no substitute. So there's a whole generation growing up with passion by proxy. Imitation passion breeds imitation people. Imitation people will mostly do what is expected, but it won't be coming from the heart; it will be coming from the head. And head rules change according to who's in power and what they need you to believe. Heart rules never change. They come from the heart, *by* the heart, and *for* the heart. Anyone can turn your head. No one can turn your heart. We are creating a whole nation of inauthentic uneccentric generic clones who are lifeless and passive. If they knew they could be who they truly are and they knew all of us were in it together and that they were part of an even larger world, they would probably want to participate in making that world a better place.

So you need a mentor. Go find one. He doesn't have to show up at your house with 3x5 cards and an outline. Your mentor can be found in a book.

Who blows your mind, who makes you come alive, whose thinking electrifies you? Whose words move you to tears? That's your mentor. You can check out every book from the library by that person and become a student all over again. If you can find a mentor-mensch in person, you're luckier than most. They're in short supply.

Don't go mentorless. If your particular teacher is not manifesting himself, maybe you can mentor yourself. All that means is accepting the position and becoming your own advocate so that you can begin to coach yourself. Pretend you, as teacher, have found the student of a lifetime. A sponge, someone who is thirsty to learn, someone you have always wanted to give everything you've got to. This student will thank you for your teachings like you have never been thanked. Don't think single apple; think entire orchard.

This teaching thing goes both ways. You can also become a mentor for someone else. As James Hillman says, "Mentoring begins when your imagination falls in love with the fantasy of another." You don't have to have some kind of special training for that. All you need is your authenticity and your eccentricity and your heart's willingness to share its fire. You need to believe what Martha Graham says: "Everyone is born a genius; it just takes some of us longer to forget." You need to remember your own brilliance. The job requires no preparation. Just show up and be real.

EXERCISES:

Find a child, a young person. Make a date with them and teach them something brand-new that is brand-new for you, too. There must be the element of excitement; it can't be faked (they've already seen enough of that). Remember, the job requires being passionate. The job doesn't involve being competent and qualified, although competence and qualification are big plusses.

Write a paragraph about someone you think might have mentored you. What did they teach you? And what are you doing with that teaching now?

Write a list of your present mentors. If the list is nonexistent, go looking. Remember: When you are ready, the teacher is there.

Think of the young people you know. Allow yourself to see more than the exterior. Do you have a special feeling about anyone you've come into contact with recently? A feeling that this person has something special, is going to be someone special, has insights and qualities different from his or her contemporaries? If you know someone like this, give that person some attention and perhaps some words of encouragement; call it part-time mentorism.

Try Not to Try Too Hard

Sing as if no one is listening
Dance as if no one is watching
Love as if you've never loved before
Submit as if you've never been rejected.

So you've done the work. You've simmered your stories. You've invited your muse. You've stayed in the present. You've listened to the silence. You've glued your seat to the seat. You've honored your process. And now, lo and behold, what have we here? A product. A piece, an article, a short story, a play, a novel. And you're ready to send it forth.

Before I was a published writer, my questions were not about writing. I don't remember asking, "How do I make my characters believable? How do I stay in my voice? Or, How do I write good endings?"

No. I'm pretty sure I asked how I could get my stuff out there and who to send it to and how to write a cover letter and if it was okay to submit the same story to many places simultaneously and anything and everything to do with getting the thing published so I could get the glory-glory-hallelujah.

If you're like me, you would prefer to have lofty thoughts about writing "just for your own pleasure," but underneath loft is always Truth. And the truth is, most of us want recognition for our efforts.

I could tell you what I know about the world of publishing, but they have whole books called *How to Publish.* After I'm finished with you, you can go to the library and sit and make copious notes.

Getting your work into the world is the thrill it looks like. But don't get it mixed up with the happily-ever-after thing: *Once someone publishes my story then I'll be happy. Once I have a book, then I'll be content. Once I have a byline, then all my dreams will be fulfilled.* The dentist will still tell you you need root canal and your tape deck in your car will still chew your favorite tape and your best friend will still move to Antarctica.

I can't tell you how to get published. I can give you a few good hints, though. Try not to try too hard. Whenever I try too hard, I ruin everything.

It's true that James Taylor didn't call and ask me what I thought of the lyrics while he was writing "Try Not to Try Too Hard," but my take on it is that of course you try. You don't lie down in the middle of the road and say, "Oh universe, how I surrender to you, and if a car hits you, bow and thank the Chevy that just rolled over your ribcage. But you have to be able to work hard and then step back and trust that whatever happens, happens. No point in planning. My grandmother had the best Yiddish expression: *man trakht und got lakhn* (man plans and god laughs).

Here is a hint for what to do if you want to get your work published in magazines.

My friend, Dede Lahmar, who was an editor at *Seventeen* magazine, says she has a secret way that might help you if you've never had anything published. Editors are looking for samples of your writing and always ask for clips of anything you have had published. How do you get clips if you haven't published yet? It's one of those Catch-22s. Dede says to write "Letters to the Editor" and get published that way. Letters to the Editor have a much greater chance of getting published, and all an editor really wants is to see a sample of your writing.

Bug them. Call them, write them, call them, and bug them. The squeaky wheel works in the magazine world. At least it always did for me. No one gets her great writing thrown out because she called too much.

Try and let go of the fruit of the action. Write and let go of it. Keep your day job and keep writing and keep submitting and keep bugging, but let go enough so you can keep your balance. Remember it's about the writing first. And second. And third. And always.

What's Your Bag of Gold?

Shiva and Shakti, the divine couple in Hinduism, are in their heavenly abode watching over the earth. They are touched by the challenges of human life, the complexity of human reactions, and the ever-present place of suffering in the human experience. As they watch, Shakti spies a miserably poor man walking down a road. His clothes are shabby and his sandals are tied together with rope. Her heart is wrung with compassion. Touched by his goodness and his struggle, Shakti turns to her divine husband and begs him to give the man some gold. Shiva looks at the man for a long moment. "My dearest wife," he says, "I cannot do that." Shakti is astounded. "Why, what do you mean, husband? You are the lord of the universe. Why can't you do this simple thing?" "I cannot give this to him because he is not yet ready to receive it," Shiva replies. Shakti becomes angry. "Do you mean to say that you cannot drop a bag of gold in his path?"

"Surely I can," Shiva replies, "but that is quite another thing." "Please, husband," says Shakti.

And so Shiva drops a bag of gold in the man's path.

The man, meanwhile, walks along thinking to himself, *I wonder if I will find dinner tonight—or shall I go hungry again?* Turning a bend in the road he sees something on the path in his way. "Aha," he says. "Look, there is a large rock. How fortunate that I have seen it. I might have torn these poor sandals of mine even further." And carefully stepping over the bag of gold, he goes on his way.

This story from Dr. Rachel Naomi Remen, *Kitchen Table Wisdom*, really resonates for me. I wrote easily and quickly. I had always thought if I can write, anyone can write. So I stepped over this large rock that seemed to always be in my way. I never bent down to look at it or touch it. I just worried about my poor sandals. It took many years for me to come home to writing, and to realize that it was my bag of gold.

I've turned my loss of all those years I could have been writing into a glass-is-half-full deal. I was even able to see the beauty of not writing until later in life. After all, you can't start playing professional basketball when you're older, you can't be a fashion model when you're older, you can't start a television broadcasting anchor career when you're older—but you *can* start writing, no matter how old you are.

So, if you, too, feel as if you are late in coming to your writing life, for whatever reason, remember there's only "late" when it applies to your dentist appointment.

When our fifteen-year-old son walked in on us dancing wildly to the Grateful Dead, he shrugged his teenage shoulders and said, "You guys are just late hippies." I said, "We're not late, we're right on time."

So don't let the time factor get to you. In fact, look at all you've been collecting. Had you known, you would have carried a notebook, huh? Okay, so maybe you're not even going to start writing now, but the notebook isn't going to hurt anything. Make it a small notebook so it fits in your jacket pocket or your bag. If you can carry a big container of moisturizer and a liter bottle of spring-water, then you can carry a little notebook. It's not a commitment. It's not an announcement—*check me out, I'm suddenly a writer.* Instead, it's a tool in case you happen to have a thought, a realization, a beginning of a story. When that little gem comes, you think you'll remember it, but I can promise you, you won't.

If you pay attention, you might notice that your creative flow happens at particular times. Does yours happen mostly when you're in your car? Do you wake up in the middle of the night with whole poems flowing out of your forehead? If you do best when you're out walking your 3.8 miles, the notebook will do you no good if it's tucked in your pocketbook waiting for you to come home. How about a little mini-cassette recorder? It might take you a few years to recognize your bag of gold, then a few more before you decide what kind of sack you'll carry it in, and a few more before you do anything about picking it up. And if you're like me, a bunch more before you actually start respecting it enough to make it happen.

What is your bag of gold? Your bag of gold can be a relationship, a job, a lifestyle change. While you've been inhaling aromotherapy, what's been sitting right under your nose?

EXERCISE:

What is your bag of gold? What has your journey been in regard to this longing?

How to Keep This Good Thing Going

At the end of my summer workshops on Thursdays at noon, the ten people who have just written their hearts "in" stay in my yard, hugging and talking and reading to each other. They have just finished a week where they wrote eight pieces—four in class and four at home at night. They've laughed, they've cried, they've spun their secrets into gold. They linger in my garden like stray kittens who've been fed warm buttermilk and don't want to be suddenly weaned on cold water and hard kibble.

"How can we keep this good thing going?" they beg me. What they want, what they are already missing—what "good thing" they want to keep going—is the feeling of being able to be who they are. They have just all allowed—no, they have just celebrated each other for being who they are. And they wrote it to prove it. No stories were too weird, no descriptions too severe, no characters too exaggerated. They wrote the truth and they didn't get hammered. They wrote the truth and they got applauded (and I don't hold up an applause sign). They wrote their own stories in their own voices, their own rhythms, from their own perspectives. They gave each other permission to have their own feelings. No one needed anything from anyone because there was always enough to go around.

This is what happens all the time—spontaneously and automatically. The bravos are love cheers for themselves as well. They are cheering for their collective humanity. They are reclaiming their right to be vulnerable. They have just reminded each other that that is when they do their best work.

When people aren't pitted against each other, when they are not even mildly competing, when people aren't vying for position (because all positions in this circle are equally important), they jump out of themselves and into their humanity. They fall so in love with each other they think they wrote each other's pieces. They're proud of each other and they root for each other. They cry for each other and they feel for each other. When people feel safe, they recognize themselves in others, and instead of being threatened by their differences, they are moved by them. When they are safe, they are moved by their *own* differences.

The world outside this safe circle has so many qualifications, so many restrictions, so many labels, boxes, judgments: You're rich, you're tall, you're young, you're beautiful, your marriage is good, your car is nice—whoops—your degrees are from the wrong school, your father didn't have the right job, your mother was a foreigner, your antiques aren't old enough, your kids haven't accomplished enough, you aren't making the right amount of money, your view of the ocean is on the wrong side, you're collecting the wrong artist, your computer is outdated, your Super Bowl seats are off by two rows, *your your your.* It's exhausting how many standards we have to live up to just for a simple piece of respect, just for a touch of validation.

Why should we be surprised? We came out of the womb and our mothers said, "Oooh look—a perfect little baby." And our fathers looked down into our puffy, filmy eyes and said, "I will love you if you're smart," and then our mothers looked again and said, "I will love you if you're pretty," and then our fathers said, "I will love you if you play football," and then our mothers said, "I will love you if you play the flute." And then our aunts came over and said, "You're not going to let her out of the house wearing her hair like that, are you?" And then our uncles came over and said, "And who do you think you are, young lady?" You were only three at the time and you looked up at this not-so-loving man and your little mind was saying to itself, *Well, I thought I was . . . but maybe that's not such a good idea. Maybe I better be . . . Who was it he wanted me to be again?* So, we learned very early how to be who they needed us to be. We learned how to accommodate, assimilate, validate them. We sang for them and we danced for them and we played football and flute for them—and we either wore our hair that way or we wore our hair this way—all for that shred of acknowledgment, that grin on our father's face when he was actually looking at us and getting a kick out of us. We learned how to work for that grin.

So, here comes the workshop, this place where, all of a sudden, who you are is the most important ingredient in the mix, rather than whether you're a great poet or a brilliant wordsmith. It's first a place where authenticity counts big time. Here you are melting the others' masks off in a ritual fire of total acceptance. So everyone trusts everyone and everyone has connected with everyone like rubber cement—close, but with a little give to it—and it's safe.

When someone slips back into being a regular human, maybe you'll hear envy—a kind of admiration envy—"Oh, I wish I could write like you, Helen." And then we all jump—an ever-so-gentle jump—on that person and say, "But you can't because you aren't Helen. And you didn't have Helen's father. Or Helen's house or Helen's indoor-outdoor carpeting." And whoever had a momentary lapse, a flash of fear, gets it.

That is not to say that all talent is the same, that no one is a better writer than anyone else. There are differences in gifts, but when there is safety, we are only hearing the one person who is reading at that moment and we are not comparing him to John Cheever or Margaret Atwood or anyone else in the class. Comparisons are nonexistent when there is no contest. And the workshop is not a contest. Creativity is not about winners and losers. If you're doin' it, you're a winner.

So when they say, "How do we keep this good thing going?" it's not just about "How do I keep writing?" It's about "How do I keep writing and feeling this good about the writing?" Do you have a guarantee that you will *always* feel good about anything? If the environment is inspirational, recovery from the slumps, blocks, and bumps takes place more quickly. Just writing will become the priority.

The most important part of your group writing life is that you are safe.

Most towns and cities have adult evening classes or continuing education or community colleges that offer creative writing courses. You don't have to take it for credit. You can take it to keep this good thing going, and you can take it to network. There are places where you can meet fellow writers and then start your own ongoing writing workshop. Put an ad in your local paper or a notice up at the bookstore you love. The most important part of the description is safety.

I was in a writing workshop when I was about thirty-six, as tender as any new writer could be. The group had been meeting for about thirteen years. I knew a few of the people, so I got up my nerve and I asked if I could join. I should have known immediately that this was going to be a "grim" fairy tale, because there was something in the way they said yes that felt like, "No, but if you prove yourself, and you're not too good and you're not too bad, we'll allow your scamy presence into our highly literary club." I didn't bring anything to read the first three weeks. They didn't ask me to read the first three weeks. The writing was very high caliber and the suggestions and comments were intelligent but very critical. I was intimidated but probably would have been intimidated even if the work had been mediocre and the people had been nice. When it was time for me to read, I didn't have the courage to try something I was insecure about and really wanted feedback on. Instead, I read something I knew was a "sure thing." Something I secretly knew was great. I needed their approval more than I needed their expertise. So I read them this piece that I had thought was so terrific and they tore it apart.

I held back the tears while the apple crisp was served and eaten. I held back the tears as I thanked everyone (what was I thanking them for, using a razor instead of an Xacto knife?), and I held back the tears while I put on my coat. But as soon as I got into the car, I cried all the way home. I did not return to the writing workshop and I did not write again for three years. Three *years,* I am telling you. Three years of thinking I was no good, a no-talent, a wanna-be—someone who would end up in the arts and crafts room of the Hebrew Home for the Aged.

Three years is a long time to give away your power to strangers that may or may not have known what they were talking about. The issue is not a question of whether my piece was good or written well or full of antecedents that didn't match their preceding pronouns. It was about common kindness, healthy communication, and a willingness to give.

I know about safety and the creative process. I know after teaching for twenty-five years that creativity needs a warm cocoon. That is not to say that you lie and tell people their stuff is great if it's not. That doesn't mean pumping people up to make them like you or say nice things about your work. It means finding the strengths *first,* the power in the work *first,* the beauty in the work *first*—and saying it out loud in front of everybody. According to one workshop veteran, I use what she calls "reverse editing." I love this description. Basically, I tell you what is great, then you feel great. Then you ask for the the things that are not great, and together we find them and we work on them.

People have said, "Yeah, but there must be times when you just can't find anything positive to say." I don't care who is writing, there is always something redeeming. If there isn't one word, one comma, one conjunction that is noteworthy, I think about what it took for this person to have written this and to have read it out loud. So I thank him for his courage, for his originality, for his honesty. What happens with people when they receive a gentle encouraging response is that their shoulders drop from their ears and their hearts open one inch more. They start to take chances: The safer they feel, the more confidence they get, and the more confidence they feel, the deeper they go. And the deeper they go, the better the writing gets.

Another reason they become better writers is that the other participants in making it safe have now become teachers. Everyone learns from everyone else. So if you want to start a writing group, make up an ad something like this:

Writing Group Forming

> This group is more about being in a safe place to write with people who are emotionally safe than it is about publishing, polishing, or picking out the problems. This is about creating, not criticism. It is about the practice of writing.

Maybe around nine people will respond. The next thing you do is meet at a public place, like a coffee shop. That way you can eliminate Hannibal Lector's protegé. Then you can start meeting at the local library, and as soon as you have a solid six or seven and you all agree that you feel ready to commit to this, you can start taking turns having it at your houses. It's best to start with meeting every two weeks because people have trouble coming every week (unless they're paying) till they know how delicious the rewards are. Then you can move it up to once a week.

The most important thing is to make two rules: safety and no disclaimers. Tell people they are allowed to say, "I didn't understand," or, "I got confused when . . ." but they aren't allowed to say, "That really sucked."

As far as disclaimers go, they can't be part of any practice. I taught at Trinity College in Hartford, Connecticut, which had at one time been all male. When I would call on the young men they would read immediately. When I would call on the female students, invariably they would look down at their paper and then say something like, "I don't think I did this right?" or, "I'm not sure if this is what you wanted?" ending in the ever-tragic question mark upspeak. After three weeks of hearing these young women, whose voices had already been stolen, whose power had already disappeared, I stopped everything and did an imitation of the boys with their sense of authority, and then the girls with their apologies for living. I said, "This is a tragedy. Your work is every bit as brilliant as theirs. But you still can't believe it. And no one else will either, if you begin with a disclaimer. Now," I told them, "when I call on you I want you to think, 'Wow, are these people lucky! They are going to hear this absolutely terrific piece of prose.' Then you may begin." Of course we all laughed, but it changed everything. Once in a great while, when someone forgot and began with a disclaimer, the whole class would hiss and boo, making sure the apologizer knew it was all in good fun. Then we would invite her to begin again.

READING YOUR WORK IN A GROUP

There are many ways to approach reading the others' writing. Some groups aren't allowed to speak after a reader has read. Some groups make copies for everyone to have so they can read them in advance. Some groups agree to giving only positive feedback (even when someone asks for criticism) for the first six months. The group will come up with a consensus. Pick your issues. What time you meet and what you serve to eat is not as important as let's write, and let's keep it safe.

If you can't go the writing group route, find just one partner and try to meet once a week (once a week is easier for two people) at different coffee shops, or trade abodes, or you can e-mail or fax or mail your work to each other. You'll know soon enough if you have chosen your partner well.

Writing partners are like marriages; they require unconditional, unjudgmental support, honesty and commitment, flexibility, and a good sense of humor. You'll probably have a better chance than most marriages because there won't be money or children involved.

EXERCISES:

Make three phone calls having to do with forming or re-forming a writing group.

Practice reading one of your pieces out loud. Include a silent affirmation just before you read:

> *I am a great writer.*
>
> *I have great courage to write.* (Don't forget, the root word of courage in French is *coeur* and it means "heart.")
>
> *This is my practice and I honor it.*
>
> *All the furniture in this house, every spider on these walls, each vegetable in that refrigerator is so lucky to be hearing these brilliant thoughts of mine.*

Great Exercises

These are some writing samples done in class and at home.

Write about a lie told to you:

Lies Laying Around

by Liz Gordon

There's the word *lying*, which means "telling stories," as my grandmother used to say, and there's lying as in resting, or is it laying? I've always confused the two. Strangely enough, telling falsehoods and reclining go together. Maybe it's because saying things that aren't true takes so much out of you.

Both were truly appropriate the day your father cozied up beside me on the comforter, his wadded-up hanky half in and half out of his breast pocket, to cautiously place his hand on my eight-month-strained abdomen. We both felt you flipping over to get comfortable in your homemade waterbed.

"I don't care if she's your top salesperson. I want her fired and out of our lives," I told him. And he kissed me and made me a promise.

That day your father and I ended one relationship and began another, but I would have to hear him make that same promise three more times before you and I left.

"You lay things down," Mrs. Edwards used to say. "It's people who lie."

Write a letter to a dead person. Here's what Laura Roosevelt did with this assignment. She had a week in which to do this.

Dead Letters

Dear George Burns,

I can't believe you finally died. I've never been particularly fond of cigars—or of you, for that matter—but I did admire your spunk.

Sincerely,

Laura

Dear Richard Nixon,

I was in my early teens when you resigned. It was in August, and my friend Brook and I and the Warnke twins were at the Martha's Vineyard Agricultural Fair. Even though you hadn't exactly come out and said so, everyone knew you were going to step down, and everyone wanted to watch you do it on TV. So I left the fair with Brook and the Warnke twins, and we crossed Music Street to a house whose television we could see was on. Even though we didn't know the people who lived there, we knocked on the door and asked whether we could watch Nixon with them, and they said sure, and ushered us into their living room.

So now you're dead, and I'm in my mid-thirties and living on Martha's Vineyard full-time, and if things work out right, I'm soon going to buy a house around the corner from the one in which I watched you resign. Small world, isn't it?

Sincerely,

Laura

Dear Eleanor Roosevelt,

The older I get, the more in awe of you I am. If I could spend a day with any dead person who ever existed, I would spend it with you.

Yours admiringly,

Laura

Dear Daddy,

I just wrote to your mother and told her that she's the dead person I'd most like to spend a day with, but now that I consider it, I think I'd rather spend that day with you. I hardly knew her in life, and I'm afraid I'd feel more like an interviewer than a granddaughter. Mind you, I'd do a lot of interviewing of you, too, to get down—on tape if you wouldn't mind—all the stories you told me that I promptly forgot because I assumed you'd always be there to tell them again.

I'd start my day with you here, on Martha's Vineyard. It would be summer, and we'd get up early and have breakfast with my husband and daughter so you could meet them. Then, we'd pack a cooler and sail the Half Moon over to that little bay at Cuttyhunk so we could swim. Then we'd be transported back to the old farm in New York, which would be as it used to be before you had to let the developers have it. We'd go for a drive so you could check on the cows and the condition of the fencing, and then we'd come home and pick some white corn from the garden, plus some of those baby carrots and radishes you liked to dip in salt for hors d'oeuvres. You'd grill some of your gargantuan cheeseburgers on the terrace for dinner, and then we'd light a fire in the library and stay up until the wee hours, playing backgammon and talking.

You'd tell me you weren't sure you approved of my moving to Martha's Vineyard. It would strike you as too risky. You were so enthusiastic about my job as a banker in New York, even though you knew I wasn't happy at it. I could never understand this until I had my own daughter; but now I see that more than anything you just wanted me to be safe. One story I remember, because you told it to me so many times, is the one about how Harry Truman offered you a job in Washington when you got out of college, but our mother made you go to law school instead.

Politics was not a secure profession, she told you, but with a law degree you would always have something to fall back on.

The thing is, though, that you never did fall back on it, never; you always preferred to try something new.

It's been thirteen and a half years since you died, and sometimes weeks go by in which I don't think of you at all. But writing this has reminded me of how much I miss you, how much I'll always miss you. I'm sure you know that it was only because I loved you so much that I sometimes had to act as though the opposite were true.

Much, much love,

Your daughter Laura

Dear Ethel DuPont,

When I was quite young and found out that you had killed yourself, I worried that people would think you had done it because of Daddy, even though you had been married to somebody else for a long time.

Years later, one night when Daddy had had too much to drink, he told me that while he was off at sea during the war, you, who had been a famous debutante, spent all your time socializing and having fun. He alluded to the possibility of other men in your life. Whether or not this was true, when he got back, your differences had become irreconcilable.

I'm sorry if this sounds bad, but I'm glad it didn't work out between you. Otherwise he wouldn't have married my mother, and there would be no me. All the same though, and even though I understand that you were manic-depressive, there's still a little part of me that worries that he might have driven you over the edge. I know how much power he had over people who loved him.

Sincerely,

Laura

Dear Granny,

Other than old, I can't remember what you looked like. I do remember that you never moved from your seat in the corner of the couch when Mummy and I visited you in New York, and that when you kissed me you left wet slicks on my cheeks that smelled like dying. But I didn't mind visiting you: You had a sweet gray Persian cat and an Irish cook who made delicious brownies.

Mummy says you were a hypochondriac and would put her to bed if she so much as sneezed. If you were so concerned about her health, how could you have failed to notice that she was being abused by her nanny? How could it have taken a concerned phone call from her teacher before you took the trouble to find out why she'd become so skittish and withdrawn, and why there were bags under her eyes?

Perhaps you were too busy with your parties. Daddy said you were a wonderful flirt and storyteller, a fun person to sit next to at dinner. Mummy says that this is all you aspired to: to be a scintillating dinner companion, particularly to men. The principal lesson you tried to teach her, she says, was the "importance of good breeding"—not so much people's behavior as their pedigrees. You talked about it with her over and over. "I made a point," she said to me once, "a deliberate point, of not passing this on to you." She told me this when we were driving together, and she was at the wheel. She never took her eyes off the road.

How could you have been so shallow? You weren't anything like my other grandmother. Mummy says that her father was terribly conservative, which I guess means that you were, too, insofar as you had any political thoughts. You must have been shocked, and not altogether pleased, by Mummy's choice of husband. And Lord knows, when I married a Jew, it probably would have killed you if you hadn't already been dead.

Mummy has always kept a framed photo of her father on the wall by her desk, but there are no pictures of you in her house. When I was six and Mummy called from New York to tell me that you had died, I sobbed and sobbed on my end of the phone, not because you were gone, but because there were tears in Mummy's voice. I had never heard her cry.

Your granddaughter,

Laura

Dear Winston Churchill,

A while ago someone gave me a poster of a Yousuf Karsh portrait of you in a dark three-piece suit. You know this photograph—the one that makes you look so stern, with the knuckles of your right hand resting on your hip, and your lower lip pushed slightly upward. A photographer told me that Karsh claimed you were pouting, since he'd reached out just before snapping the photo and snatched your cigar from your lips.

Anyway, I had this poster framed, and I hung it across from

the bathroom in the hallway of our old apartment in New York. Since I am in the habit of leaving the bathroom door open unless there are guests around, it always felt as though you were summing me up when I was on the john.

Now we're renting a house, and the poster of you is in storage. But still, sometimes I have that self-conscious feeling when I pee, so rest assured that you're here with us in spirit.

Fondly,

Laura

P.S. By the way, George Burns died recently. He liked cigars, too. Small world, isn't it?

This exercise starts with the line:

I never want to be so earthbound that I can't . . .

Imagine the stars falling out of the sea and landing as tear drops on my face

by Carol Goldberg

"I'm depressed," Lars said. "I need a friend, come with me—we'll stay for an hour and then you can go home." It sounds all right to me. He talks and feels less depressed; I listen and feel more worthwhile. That balmy, autumn evening I tell him that maybe his depression is because he is sitting on his desire—he loves this new way of looking at the issue—the issue being that he may lose his home if he doesn't come up with mortgage money. Lars had been paralyzed up to this point as to how he really felt about losing the dark T Street row house, and our conversation had put him in touch with his real yearnings. So here we are at this art fund-raising party, and Martha announces that the publication has been around for 22 years. Connections and relationships seem to have jumped into the double digits. Lars and I have been friends for 10 years, Hank and I have been married for 35 years, I have 3 adult kids that are all over 29 years. I look around the room, feeling heavy under the pileup of time. I see a couple of artists that I have known since the Corcoran days. I make eye contact, and when their eyes roll across my face, I make a decision to hate them. I like how energized I suddenly feel, and remember when energy, desire, and passion were at the tips of my fingers . . . when these feelings were unrelated to immovable objects.

I drop Lars off, feeling good about our interconnection, but it's midnight and I'm anxious to smell my studio. I walk in, flick on the lights and look around at the particles of grown-up matter neatly lining the walls and shelves. I sniff the air, remembering the art-school aroma of turpentines, oils, and clays. Now, my reds are made from acrylic, pastels, or gouache, and the limbic system is left straining. I worry that I am infusing the moments of the night with more drama than truth, and I tell myself, Hey, it's late, go to bed—tomorrow is another day.

Hank is already in bed trying to get drowsy on the Discovery Channel. A pack of hyenas play out a Shakespearean drama on the tube as they circle a gracefully confused gazelle. I enter the bedroom and wonder if my whole life is really about being in this room. Years ago, when I told my mother that I was going back to school for art, she was struck with fear that I could work too hard, lose interest in my family, abandon my husband, and neglect my kids.

"Would your grandmother have left your grandfather alone in the bedroom to carouse in Krakow?" I imagined she asked.

"Bubbala," I picture my grandmother saying to me as she slips into bed beside Grandpa, "Bubbala, get into bed, forget the strangers, that's not where you belong."

Grandma predates the big bang. She was born practicing the unified field theory. She knew at any given micro-minute that her family came first, that her career was her husband, and that her ambition was for the *kinder.* You couldn't separate those ideas—they stuck together and spun within the nucleus of Grandma's soul. My mother inherited that universe, and I felt the force of that tradition. I slide into bed next to Hank. I think of ourselves as tiny particles—*hadrons*—gently bumping into each other in our supercollider, king-sized bed. I like hadrons because I read somewhere that their interaction at close range is one hundred times stronger than the electromagnetic interaction at the same distance. We are charged as lightning, as electrified as that TV set. My toes search for his toes. I miss him and want to feel his coolness. As he slips his arm behind my shoulder, I close my eyes and see Grandma dancing under the light of a tiny photon. She flutters over to the bed and kisses the stars that spin in the teardrops on my face.

Glenn A. Bergenfeld has taken my workshop a few times. Usually there are nine women and him. Maybe it's because he talks about his wife and two daughters with such respect and love that we are able to appreciate and laugh at the things he writes, but more likely it's because they're stunning. This is the lie he wrote:

> "I got this scar during the Vietnam War," I told her. I pointed to my eyebrow and forehead. I was drinking Scotch, again, and I was back in grad school, again, waiting for the Great American Novel to pass through me.
>
> What I'd said to her was, strictly speaking, a fact. What I didn't care to disclose was that I'd gotten the scar not in Da Nang, but in Indiana in 1974 when, in a fit of rage, I'd deliberately smashed my face against the steering wheel of my Volkswagen. And that wasn't even the strange part. Next, with my own blood dripping into my mouth (a strange taste), I'd taken my bug up to ninety-five miles per hour—top speed—cranked open the moonroof, and with the cornfields of the Midwest passing by in a blur, I'd jerked off into an athletic sock while a trucker in the right lane watched me. He must have had a CB because by the time I came, there was a convoy of Marlboro-smoking, horn-tooting perverts drowning out any exclamation of pleasure that might have burped out of me. Oh, like you guys never jerked off on the interstate? Sure.
>
> If it sounds like there's a woman behind this bad deportment and she was unable to meet my needs, that she didn't honor our differences, then you're a fucking genius.
>
> I could tell you just one thing about her and you'd see how I ended up on the interstate, bloodied and with only one sock that I could wear. She had this disease or condition called Renault's phe-

nomenon. The capillaries in her extremities were too small or her hands didn't have enough electricity or something, and her hands were always freezing. Even if she just heard that it was cold somewhere else, her hands would get all cold and lifeless. They'd turn purple when it was really cold and get tiny cuts on them. It was pretty horrible.

She was pretty horrible, too. Always complaining. Everything was unfair to her. And her gender, though she didn't have any female friends. Thought women were bitchy, can you imagine?

Was it Tolstoy who got his work done between trips to the sanitarium to drop off or pick up his wife? With women and art there's Cheever at one extreme. He kept working because women, even his daughters, took care of him. Then there's Tolstoy, who took care of his woman and wrote a novel. And there's me. Can't get my woman to go to the sanitarium but can't write my novel because she's making so much noise at home.

One night she'd made me so crazy I'd just bolted. Gone out and fallen asleep on some rich guy's soft, green lawn. I woke up when his dog, in mid-crap, saw me and decided barking at a bum beat his usual morning shit. I ran for it. I wandered around town. Had a hot dog at ten-thirty. By eleven-thirty I'd bought a movie ticket. Since this was the South—Chapel Hill—the only matinee was, of course, *Gone With the Wind.*

I went in, and I was the only one there. That is, until this guy came and sat next to me. Now there were two of us in this huge theater. Scarlett was being especially hard on the darkies and her men. Though I'd never seen the movie, I knew that she gets hers—

they burn the bitch out of her house and she ends up wearing the curtains. What a stitch!

But I was not to see that, since the guy next to me began to press his leg against mine.

He hadn't even looked at me. I could have had warts, tattoos, even my own excrement on my face. But I saw that his dick was about to burst his zipper and he thought it was all for me, but it wasn't. It was for the idea of me. It was for hiding in the dark, coming in the movie house, while the fag-bashers are working as loan officers at the bank next door. If we ever learn to accept them, the lights will go out. They'll become just like us and they'll fight more than they fuck.

Which is what I would say to her every night after class. "Fuck or fight?" I'd follow her around the house. "Fuck or fight? Fuck or fight?" I'd ask until she gave me the finger. But she meant fight.

I left *Gone With the Wind* and headed home.

In a great break with tradition, I changed the refrain. "Where's my Tigers hat?" I asked. "And my Martha's Vineyard sweatshirt?" She'd commandeered this stuff early on, like so much booty from a war. I started to grab my stuff and just fling it into the car. We were fighting in and out of the house, on the walkway, through the car and over the hood. She even threw in some records and I screamed they weren't mine and threw them onto the lawn and she got them and said "fuck you" and threw them back into my car, but she was a klepto and she took them from our friend Curtis and I said, "Fuck me? Fuck me? Fuck you, you demon bitch from hell." Then she started to smile, but I didn't, and then she started to laugh. It was a pretty funny scene. She'd always gone first. She'd picked me. She'd gotten us to move out on this fucking farm so I could write. She started fighting first and she went crazy first.

And now she was over it first. And over me, just like that. I needed to go somewhere and have my own ceremony, jerk her out of me alone, anonymously, without her watching.

So I consider the woman across from me. She's drinking Scotch. The drink of serious novelists—a good sign. Maybe she won't drive me crazy and I'll get my book done. I don't tell her my stupid story about being captured by Viet Cong. I figure that this is her third (fourth?) Scotch. And I consider the writer's sacred duty to tell the truth.

"After the war," I say, "I was drinking tequila, in Guanajuato, Mexico . . . minding my own business, and some piss-smelling, shit-for-brains cop bashed me with his rifle and dragged me to jail. He was screaming, 'CIA, CIA, you motherfucker.' I still don't know why."

One of the assignments I give that always works is *Write about a time when you felt one way and acted another*. Here is the one Susan Block wrote:

I have been seeing my therapist for about four months. I am beginning to feel comfortable and safe. It is somewhere toward the end of one of my sessions that I am responding to her question, "So, who are you?"

"Well, I'm a forty-eight-year-old married woman, mother of two kids, vegetarian, nonsmoker. I don't drink. I love hiking, biking, swimming, cross-country skiing; I like to write, play the piano, work in my garden, take photographs. . . ." I pause for a second in contemplation of what to say next.

"Do you masturbate?" she asks.

Instantly I know who I am. I am an emotional furnace. I'm burning up. Every ounce of blood rushes into my face. This must be what they call the hot seat. I scrunch up my nose and mouth and make a face of disgust. "No, it's not for me," I defend.

I am totally rattled. She said the word I have yet to pronounce, and she wants to know if I do it? I look at the clock. There's a short time left to the session. I've got to get out of here. I grab the photograph book that I had brought in to share. I dare not look directly at my therapist, but with my peripheral vision I am able to see that she is still sitting serenely and stately, legs crossed, hands relaxed across her lap, and she's not even slightly tinted in the face. For someone who just said the *M* word, her composure is one of sainthood. I wish I could mirror her calmness, but—"I've really got to get going," I quickly say, and with head down, I look at the nubby beige carpet and head for the door. . . .

Once outside, I breathe in the cool air to extinguish the blazing furnace of heat that is racing through my body, and quickstep it to the safety of my car.

Masturbation. I pull down a book from the middle shelf at B. Dalton bookstore. I am standing under the capital letters that read: HUMAN SEXUALITY. I skim my fingers through the *M*'s in the index . . . mantras, marriage, martial arts, massage cream and oils; I push the book back and pull down the next. The cover's dull. . . . I return it to its place. I reach up at random. A pink and white covered book slides into my hand. *Sex for One*, by Betty Dodson. I let the pages fall left and right where they may. My eyes read, ". . . but the most consistent sex you will have in your life is the love affair with yourself. Sexual healing begins by learning how to turn yourself on, discover your fantasies and give yourself an abundance of self-love and orgasms." Wow! I don't have to look at the index. This book is masturbation. I glance through the aisle toward the checkout counter. The clerk is alone. I never saw her before; she doesn't know me; there are no familiar customers in sight. Quickly, I semi-jog to the desk, place the book and my money down in one nervous motion and then proceed to thumb through the tiny calendars at arm's length of the register while she calculates the cost and wraps my book. Moments later . . . alone in my car at last, I breathe.

I know my therapist well enough to know that she won't let me off the hook. No, it's not that she will convince me to "do it," but she will suggest that we examine my immediate negative response and ask, "How come?" So I decide I had better update myself on this "not for me" activity and read about something of which I know little.

I am at home. It is nine P.M. I prop two pillows behind my head and begin to read. My eyes take in the first few sentences. Fifty-two pages later, I haven't skipped over one word or missed a single erotic illustration. I am feeling that this is the best plotless book I have ever read.

It is exactly one week later; I am in New York City at West 57th

Street. The book says that I will find it at Eve's Garden. I walk up two flights of stairs and enter the sex shop. In that moment, I know that I cannot say when asked, "I'm browsing." It seems too invasive to even look. A female form comes into view. I hear the words.

"May I help you?" She is moving in my direction. She looks like a librarian; she could be a librarian; I tell myself I need to imagine that I am talking with a librarian.

"Oh, I was just . . ."

I stop speaking.

"I mean, yes, I am looking for something, but I'm not sure what I want because I've never had one. It . . ."

She senses my nervousness.

"It's okay," she says. "You probably have never been in a store like this before, have you?"

"No, never, and well, I read Betty Dodson's book . . ."

She finishes my sentence, ". . . and you want to buy a vibrator."

"Yes, yes, but I don't know anything about them."

"That's okay. Here, let me show you a few of them and their different features, and then you can decide."

Oh, God, I pray no one walks in the store. How do I nonchalantly look at vibrators? I think to myself.

". . . and this one runs on batteries, but it's sort of noisy. This one is good for traveling. This one—"

"How about the one she talks about in the book?" I ask.

"Oh, the Magic Wand—quite good, quite reliable."

The tension is building within me. Suddenly it blurts out. "I'm new at masturbating."

She takes it as though I have just said, "I'll have chicken on rye."

"Many women haven't until they read *Sex for One*," she replies.

My coat of ice is melting; my shield of armor softens. Something is happening because I begin to turn my head and look around.

"I'll take the Magic Wand," I say with some element of trust. "Do you think I need anything else?"

Two bottles of lubricant later and a G-spotter attachment for the Magic Wand, I am feeling, This is unbelievable. . . . What a great store.

"What about one of those?" I bravely say, pointing to a dildo.

"I'd wait," she says with compassion.

Little does she know that she could sell me one of everything in the shop. Where have I been? I lament to myself.

So, smugly, serendipitously, and skittishly, I leave the store, the proud owner of a Magic Wand vibrator, and having practically memorized with ease the first ninety-two pages of Betty Dodson's book, I am ready. . . .

And so it is, back at home in the confines of a warm and tiny room, that little Miss Proper, do everything right, who doesn't smoke or drink, finally vibrates. The steam steams, the pot boils, the lid pops its top all at once. In one magic moment, I have an incredible love affair with myself, and in the reflective moments afterwards, I plan the rest of my life in terms of rainy days, lonely nights, morning quickies—and spontaneous desires—just me and my vibrator.

Weeks later, I return to therapy after an extended holiday break. I plop the book *Sex for One* down in front of my therapist.

"I have a new compulsive behavior. . . . I'm really into it," I beam.

"What's *it*?" she asks.

My once crunched-up face of disgust is now one big, happy grin, and in that moment she loses her place of neutrality and composure and together . . . we laugh.

On the last day of the four-day workshop, people are spent, drained, happy, catatonic, high as kites on acid, raring to go, mellow. I give them something easy, like *Write about something you're wearing right now.* Lori A. Roth wrote:

Shorts

I'm wearing a pair of cut-off shorts, made when the blown-out knees of my jeans spread to gaping flaps and a knotty mass of loose thread. I love these shorts, take pains to stitch the splitting seams and fraying buttonholes along the fly—let them carry me through another sticky summer.

I remember when I bought them in a small French boutique on the East Side. I came in wearing standard Levi's, a little baggy in the seat. I was mousier then, and tried to stay small as I thumbed through the sale rack, browsing. I had no business in this store, I thought. Nothing here for someone like me.

There they were: $35 and a wild cartoon facing that only I would know about. Perhaps it was the secret, or the way they rode the curve of my hips, but somehow these jeans had a pulse. I paid cash.

I'm a woman of many moods and many moments and even

when I feel good in my body I may bury it in cloth. I can see my mother frowning, saying, "You need a belt," and I wonder if her level of need is on a par with our needs for food, clothing, and shelter. She feels I need a husband, too, and somehow a flash of hip couldn't hurt. But the mood's got to be right.

It comes, and when I least expect it, though often on muggy city mornings, when leaving my damp brownstone is actually better than staying. It may be only a paper or a quart of milk I need, but that's enough—enough to pull them on and cuff them just above the knee. If I'm lazy, I throw on a loose T-shirt that breaks at the hips. If I'm polished, then I tuck it in and add the black Mexican belt with nickel studs and buckle and thick silver rings to match. And if I'm really saucy, a cropped little Spandex top for a shock of downy stomach in front and rippling spine behind. On days like that, I kinda' slide to the newsstand, no place else I'd rather go. On days like that, my hips just tick.

You see Ma, you need more than a belt—you need rhythm.

Frances Reed wrote this in fifteen minutes. The assignment was *Write about a kitchen.*

It took me four hours or more to cook myself through to the dinner guests and count their mouths by the handfuls of string beans, chummy striped bass, and pear tatin. The glass serving plates are covered up by wobbly tins and I must remember to get those down, too, and to turn the grill off and panfry tofu just plain in a darkened skillet for the kids. Meanwhile, the caterpillar has spun its cocoon hanging by a web on the underside of the green-lidded canister and has lost its head. I sit down to the long-armed humans and the growing demands to pass things. I sit long enough to catch the rare shadows from the crammed ceramic and glass and as I sit, I come to know the length of my food.

These are a few of the thousands of beautifully written pieces that have been done in my workshops with almost no time to prepare. Because there was an environment of shared safety, these writers mined for and found and then spun their stories into pure gold.

Repeat After Me

So who can write?
You can write.
And why do we write?
We write to tell the truth.
We write to know who we are.
We write to find our voices.
We write to save the world.
We write to save ourselves.
We write so that when we look back and see that moment when we were totally clear, completely brilliant and astoundingly wise, there is proof—proof right there on the page.
And we can read our words and say, "I wrote that."
And if we did it once—we can do it again.

Our deepest fear is not that we are inadequate.

Our deepest fear is that we are powerful beyond measure.

It is our Light, not our Darkness, that frightens us.

We ask ourselves, who am I to be brilliant, gorgeous, talented, fabulous?

Actually who are you NOT to be?

You are a child of God. Your playing small does not serve the world.

There is nothing enlightened about shrinking so that other people won't feel insecure around you.

We were born to make manifest the glory of God that is within us.

It is not just in some of us; it is in everyone.

And as we let our light shine, we unconsciously give other people permission to do the same.

As we are liberated from our own fear, our presence automatically liberates others.

—NELSON MANDELA